# EASTERN
# PASSAGE

# FARLEY MOWAT

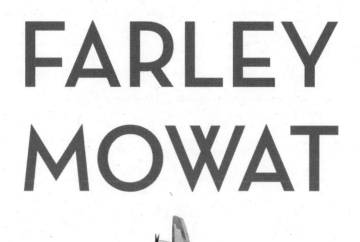

# EASTERN PASSAGE

McClelland & Stewart

**Library and Archives Canada Cataloguing in Publication**

Mowat, Farley, 1921-

Eastern passage / Farley Mowat.
Issued also in electronic format.

ISBN 978-0-7710-6491-3

1. Mowat, Farley, 1921-. 2. Mowat, Farley, 1921- – Travel – Saint Lawrence
River. 3. Atomic bomb – Accidents – Saint Lawrence River – History.
4. Nuclear accidents – Environmental aspects – Saint Lawrence River – History.
5. Environmental disasters – Saint Lawrence River – History. 6. Authors, Canadian
(English) – 20th century – Biography. I. Title.

PS8526.O89Z463 2010    C818'.5409    C2010-902284-X

Published simultaneously in the United States of America by McClelland & Stewart
Ltd., P.O. Box 1030, Plattsburgh, New York 12901

Library of Congress Control Number: 2010923466

We acknowledge the financial support of the Government of Canada through the
Book Publishing Industry Development Program and that of the Government of
Ontario through the Ontario Media Development Corporation's Ontario Book Initiative.
We further acknowledge the support of the Canada Council for the Arts and the
Ontario Arts Council for our publishing program.

Typeset in Berkley Book by M&S, Toronto
Printed and bound in Canada

ANCIENT FOREST
FRIENDLY

This book is printed on acid-free paper that is 100% recycled,
ancient-forest friendly (100% post-consumer waste).

McClelland & Stewart Ltd.
75 Sherbourne Street
Toronto, Ontario
M5A 2P9
www.mcclelland.com

1 2 3 4 5    14 13 12 11 10

# THANKSGIVING

With more than forty books behind me, the time is ripe for paying homage to those at the heart of my life and labours.

Helen and Angus Mowat, my parents, who lit the fire and kept it stoked as long as they lived.

Peter Davison, poet of note, my editorial mentor and shepherd through almost four decades.

Jack McClelland, publisher par excellence, who would – and did – do anything to keep this writer's boat afloat.

Claire Mowat, my wife and partner, who has propped me up, goaded me on, and borne with me for half a century.

Mary Talbot, unsung amanuensis who saw to it that I stayed on track and who was instrumental in delivering the goods.

Susan Renouf, infallible literary midwife and editorial helmsman, who has kept me on course these past two decades.

Albert, Victoria, Lily, Edward, Tom, Millie, and Chester, and all my friends, human and Otherwise, whose existence has made mine possible . . . and wonderful.

*Farley Mowat*
*Cape Breton Island*
*November 2010*

# AUTHOR'S NOTE

*Eastern Passage* is the second half of a memoir about my life from early 1937 to mid-1954, but excluding the Second World War. *Otherwise*, published in 2008, covers the first part of the story.

Together these two books give an account of voyages of discovery that go to the heart of who and what I was during my apprentice years as a writer. Although they revisit some events and circumstances already described in earlier books of mine, I make no apology for the reappearance (if in a new guise) of material that is essential to my tale.

# PREFACE

I returned to civilian life in 1946 having served almost five years in the Canadian Army, most of that time in the infantry. Driven by a desperate need to escape the black devils of that ordeal, I fled to the Saskatchewan prairies of my childhood, but the solace and the healing I sought were not to be found in my own past. That winter, however, I chanced upon some dusty government publications that gave me hope. They recounted how, early in the summer of 1893, a young Toronto geologist, Joseph Tyrrell, and his brother James set off to fill some of the yawning gaps in the existing maps of Canada's northern regions.

Paddled by native voyageurs, the Tyrrell brothers travelled into a world virtually unknown to white men. Ominously called the Barren Lands, it embraced an enormous expanse of tundra sprawling north of present-day Saskatchewan and Manitoba all the way to the shore of the Arctic Ocean.

In the course of three epochal journeys into it, the Tyrrells encountered such multitudes of the arctic reindeer called caribou as to make a mockery of the name Barren Lands. James wrote, "The deer could only be reckoned in acres and square miles. Joseph estimated that just *one* of the innumerable herds they saw contained as many as two hundred thousand individuals."

Equally remarkable was their discovery that the supposedly barren lands were home to as many as two thousand Inuit.

These were a people out of time. Most had never before even seen a white man, and they knew next to nothing of the sea-mammal and saltwater world that sustains most Inuit cultures. The inland people took *their* sustenance from the caribou, around which their lives revolved.

Engrossed in studying and mapping the land's geological features, Joseph Tyrrell had little time to spare for the people he met, but James, the more perceptive of the two, wrote that he wished he could have lived "with the Caribou Esquimaux" long enough to have learned how they managed to be "so happily content with their simple lives."

James Tyrrell's "wish" was reborn in me – tenfold. I was fired by a consuming desire to meet these extraordinary beings and through them perhaps find a way into an earlier and better world than the hellish one from which I had just emerged.

In January of 1947, I heard about an American zoologist who wished to spend a summer in the Barren Lands and was looking for a Canadian associate. I got in touch with him and before long had committed myself to becoming half of the "Keewatin Zoological Expedition" – the other half being Dr. Francis Harper.

The doctor wanted to spend the coming summer collecting (which is to say, killing) any non-human living things that could be converted into scientific specimens, whereas I wanted to find and follow the great deer herds into the country of the Caribou Esquimaux.

In mid-May Harper and I boarded a train, which ran erratically and very, very slowly north from Winnipeg to the west coast of Hudson Bay. The Muskeg Special, as the train was called, deposited us and our gear at Churchill, where I located a bush pilot willing to fly us into the Barrens.

He landed us near a trapper's cabin at remote Nueltin Lake belonging to a trio of Metis brothers who, although struck almost dumb by our surprise arrival, made us welcome.

A few weeks later, twenty-three-year-old Charlie Schweder, eldest of the Metis brothers, and I embarked on an epic canoe journey of more than a thousand miles through taiga and tundra during which I met the remnants of the Tyrrells' Esquimaux – the *Ihalmiut* – *People from Beyond* – as they called themselves.

Fewer than fifty of them still existed.

That summer was a healing time for me and one that made me hunger for more experience of Arctic lands.

At the end of that summer, I returned to Toronto, where I persuaded Andy Lawrie, a friend from pre-war days, to join me in spending a year studying the ways of the caribou and of the people of the caribou. We set about obtaining the mandatory official permission for an expedition into the Northwest Territories. This went well, and by October prospects looked very rosy. They looked even rosier to me after I met Frances Thornhill, a blond, blue-eyed veteran of the Women's Naval Service, three years younger than I.

One bright autumnal day, I took her birdwatching, and we ended up making love in a windrow of fallen leaves. A month later she confronted me, white-faced and tense, with a demand that we get married, and at once. In the language of the day, this meant she was pregnant.

The effect on my plans was not as disruptive as it might have been. Once my panic had simmered down I concluded that, although marriage might complicate things for the moment, it would bring an end to aloneness.

The pregnancy turned out to be a false alarm but we got married anyway, though we knew it would entail a separation of three or four months before Andy and I established a firm base where Fran could join us.

We were married just before Christmas of 1947. A few weeks later, Andy and I were summoned to Ottawa by the deputy commissioner of the Northwest Territories who was, for all intents and purposes, the reigning monarch of Canada's northern wilderness. Assuming we were to receive the official approval for our expedition, we hurried to the capital city and were escorted into the presence of Deputy Commissioner R.A. Gibson, a man who seemed to possess the combined persona of Captain Bligh and Colonel Blimp.

He did all the talking.

Having informed us that the Department of Mines and Resources (of which he was also the deputy minister) had decided to undertake its own study of *Rangifer arcticus* (the Barren Land Caribou) and of "the native tribes associated with this animal," he delivered the *coup de grâce*.

"You will of course understand that *your* proposal cannot now be endorsed, and the requisite Explorers and Scientists Licence to undertake fieldwork in the Northwest Territories will not be granted."

He paused to let this sink in.

"Nevertheless, my assistant tells me there may be some employment available for you. Good day, gentlemen."

His assistant "gave us the form" in proper military style.

"There are openings for two student assistants. The salary is minimal, as befits your qualifications. However, you will have the opportunity to associate with and learn from experts in the field, which I am sure you will appreciate. . . . We must have your decision today."

Andy and I spent several hours in a beer parlour glumly pondering other possibilities, but when we did return to Toronto it was as government servants. But the situation was not as bad as it seemed. Although the Department of Mines and Resources had pre-empted our original plans, we would at least be able to implement some of them – or so we hoped.

In mid-May, we travelled to Churchill, where Gunnar Ingebritson, the young owner-pilot of a beat-up Norseman bush plane, was waiting to fly us to the cabin at Nueltin Lake.

When we arrived at Windy Cabin, we found the place abandoned and the Schweders gone from the country. However, almost as soon as we moved in we were inundated by the Ihalmiut, who were in desperate straits after a starvation winter. We gave them all the food and ammunition we could spare and then began our work. Andy's designated task was to study the northbound caribou migration, while mine was to observe wolf–caribou interaction.

Learning from the Ihalmiut that, in late summer, hordes of caribou congregated around Angikuni Lake in the central Barrens, we decided to join the animals there. When Gunnar returned, bringing us a canoe and the rest of our supplies, we arranged for him to ferry us to Angikuni in mid-July.

Gunnar brought mail. My share included two letters from my wife that I immediately tore open – and wished I hadn't.

Although she had not objected to my going north and had sent me off cheerfully enough, she now saw things differently. Her letters suggested I had deliberately chosen to negate our marriage and had no intention of ever returning to it, or her. There was very little time for me to decide what to do. Bad weather was brewing and Gunnar had to return immediately to his base. I gave him a hurriedly scrawled letter for Fran in which I assured her we *would* be together in three or four months and watched him fly away.

Gunnar returned on July 10, his Norseman so laden with drums of avgas for the long flight to Angikuni that there was barely room aboard for Andy and me; for an Inuk named Ohoto, who wanted to revisit his birthplace near Angikuni; and for Tegpa, a bouncy husky pup given me by the Ihalmiut.

During the next month and a half, we four lived and travelled amongst caribou and wolves in a part of the country that, in the Tyrrells' time, had been home to at least a thousand inland Inuit. The deer were still present, though in much reduced numbers, but almost the only signs of human presence were mossed-in stone tent circles and seemingly numberless graves.

None of us was sorry (and Ohoto was ecstatic) the day a tiny flicker of metallic dust in the high sky resolved itself into Gunnar's Norseman come to carry us back to Windy Cabin. He had again brought letters from my wife. This time I opened them with dread. They were distillations of misery and despair whose overall burden was that our marriage had been a dreadful mistake and was now effectively over.

As we flew back to Windy Cabin, Andy urged me to continue on to Churchill with Gunnar, then make my way to Toronto. He assured me he would keep things going in my absence and have everything ready for Fran if I could persuade her to return with me. For his part, Gunnar assured me he had friends at the Fort Churchill airbase who might get me on a military flight to Ontario.

That evening I was in Churchill and next morning on my way east to rejoin my wife. Her reception of me was equivocal. Although she embraced me passionately, she did not repudiate her earlier conclusion that marriage to me had been a mistake. I do not know what brought about her change of mind, but before the week was out we were on a train together bound for Winnipeg, and two days later the Muskeg Special delivered us to Churchill.

On September 9 Gunnar flew us to Windy Cabin.

Flights to Nueltin tended to be hairy. This one was especially so. We had barely taken off when a whiteout almost obscured the world from view, forcing Gunnar to fly within a few yards of the rock-strewn tundra, and causing Fran to lacerate her palms from clenching her fists in fear of certain death.

After three hours of this, we splashed down on Windy Bay. Fran never did tell me what her feelings were as she peered through the cracked Plexiglas windscreen into a rain- and snow-swept vista of black water and treeless tundra. If the environs of her new home were hardly prepossessing, the log shanty awaiting her must have been appalling. Andy was never much of a housekeeper and during my absence had been almost continuously hosting Ihalmiut men desperate for ammunition with which to start the caribou hunt, for without a successful hunt the coming winter would be bleak.

The cabin's dark interior must have looked and smelled to Fran more like a bear's den than a human habitation. During the days that followed, Andy and I were preoccupied keeping tabs on the caribou herds and their ever-attendant wolves as these flowed past Windy Bay on their long trek south to spend the winter inside the taiga forests. Fran was equally busy coping with the problems of setting up a household under conditions that might have daunted a lumber-jack; in looking after a further succession of Ihalmiut visitors; and in tentatively exploring the alien world around her. In this, she was aided by Tegpa, who had claimed her as his own and would hardly leave her side.

The primitive shortwave radio issued to us had failed, leaving us with no connection to the outside world, so we had no way of finding out when Gunnar would be coming back for us, nor could we tell him of a change in *our* plans. We had all originally intended to spend the winter studying the wolves and caribou at Brochet, a village farther south in Northern Manitoba, but Andy had since decided to return to university and now planned to fly out to Churchill with Gunnar after he had delivered Fran and me to Brochet.

# · 1 ·

## IN FROM THE COLD

We had been waiting almost a month for Gunnar's plane when, on the first day of October, I stepped out of the cabin to find the nearby gravel ridges alive with dense flocks of ptarmigan making their way south ahead of winter. When I paddled off to haul the net upon which we were now largely dependent for food, I had to break through a scum of ice that had formed overnight. There could be no doubt about it – if we were not picked up within the next few days, we would be marooned for another six or seven weeks until, and if, a ski-equipped plane could land on the frozen bay.

We woke on October 9 to a falling thermometer, a plunging barometer, and a sky darkening with snow clouds. A storm was brewing, and even the usually irrepressible Tegpa was reluctant to go outside until, just before noon, he flung himself at the cabin door in a paroxysm of barking.

Seconds later the Norseman roared low over the crest of the Ghost Hills and slammed down on Windy Bay, its floats shattering the skim ice like a hardball smashing a plate-glass window. Gunnar had finally arrived. Although more than a month late, he offered no explanation or apology. When I pressed for one, he replied casually:

"Pranged a drifting oil barrel on take-off a while back. Buggered a float and this old bitch pretty near sank. Took a while to patch her up. But what the hell, let's get the show on the fuckin' road!"

Time was always of the essence with Gunnar. I heaved our gear (it didn't amount to much) on board, while Fran and Tegpa squeezed into the cramped little cabin even as Gunnar began opening the throttle and Andy shouted his goodbyes.

"Gonna be tight gettin' to Brochet before dark," Gunnar yelled to Fran and me. "Might have to spend the night on some godforsaken moose pond the middle of nowhere. But what the hell, there's a bottle of rum in the back pocket of my seat. Have yourselves a snort . . . just don't be givin' that damn dog none! Don't want no drunken dog aboard!"

Fran and I got a close-up of the world below us that day because there was a head wind to deal with, and in order to conserve gas Gunnar kept the Norseman, as he said later, "close enough to the goddamn trees if they'd been cherry trees we coulda' picked a goddamn basketful."

We flew on, fighting the wind while a shaggy carpet of spruce and Jack pine dotted with lakes and fragmented by streams and rivers slid by close beneath. Then abruptly we were over open water and Gunnar was shouting that this was Reindeer Lake.

A hundred and fifty miles long and fifty wide, contained by several thousand miles of convoluted shoreline, Reindeer Lake was the centre of the ancestral wintering ground for what in 1948 may have been as many as a quarter of a million Barren Ground caribou. The area was also home to about three hundred humans – Woodland

Crees, Chipewyans (Dene), Metis, and a scattering of white trappers. There were only two settlements – a small one at the appropriately named South End, and Brochet, only slightly larger and at the north end.

Brochet was not much to look at as Gunnar slammed the plane down on the bay in front of the settlement. Two dozen log shanties squatted haphazardly along half a mile of sandy foreshore and three sketchily fenced compounds enclosed a handful of frame structures. Two of the compounds were owned by competing trading firms; the third belonged to the Roman Catholic mission and boasted a grand new church, the glitter of whose sixty-foot steeple encased in sheet metal could be seen miles away.

Having visited Brochet on two previous occasions, I was not dismayed. Frances may have been, but was so relieved to have escaped from the Barren Lands and at finding herself comfortingly surrounded by trees again that not even the coolness of our reception daunted her.

We clambered ashore under the glacial gaze of foxy-faced and soutane-clad Fr. André Darveaux, second-in-command of the Roman Catholic mission; aging Jim Cummins, a former trapper who was now the game warden for a region encompassing about fifty thousand square miles; and willowy Jim Johnson, clerk of a trading post belonging to an entrepreneur named Isaac Schieff, who lived several hundred miles farther south. Neither of Brochet's most prominent residents – Bill Garbut, the long-time manager of the Hudson's Bay Company's sprawling, white-painted, red-roofed trading post, and white-haired Fr. Joseph Egenolf, head of the mission and the uncrowned king of the Reindeer Lake country – was in evidence.

Nominally, Brochet's population included about 250 aboriginals and people of mixed blood, but most of these spent the better part of the year widely dispersed at fishing stations and winter camps. The day we arrived, fewer than two dozen were at the settlement and none showed any desire to be friendly with Fran or me, though they did seem much taken by Tegpa, whose impressive appearance and assured behaviour was in marked contrast to that of their own dogs.

Brochet possessed two of the three elements that made up the ruling triumvirate of most northern Canadian communities in those days. The missionaries and traders were well established, but the usually ubiquitous detachment of Royal Canadian Mounted Police was absent. There were, however, two soldiers of the Royal Canadian Corps of Signals operating a weather station as part of an extensive surveillance system being constructed across the top of the continent to contain the godless communists of the Soviet Union. As a recent survivor of the Second World War bitterly averse to being sucked into another world holocaust, I would have kept my distance from the "weather station" had not my employer decreed otherwise.

A letter from the federal Department of Mines and Resources had been awaiting my arrival at Brochet. From it I learned that Andy and I (no mention made of my wife) were to winter with the soldiers in a small barracks attached to the station. However, when I approached the corporal in charge about this he told me *he* was under strict orders to deny civilian access to his high-security installation. The most he was prepared to do was let me send a radiogram to my department, apprising my employer of the situation and asking for instructions.

These came four days later, brusquely ordering me to make my own arrangements. Fran was indignant – though I was not.

"Typical SNAFU," I told her. "Situation Normal All Fucked Up. Fact is, we're probably *lucky* to be left to our own devices."

She was not easily reassured, or perhaps she glimpsed an opportunity.

"They don't seem to care what happens to us. Mightn't it be best if you resigned the job and we just went on home?"

"I'm not going to do that, Fran. The cement heads have screwed up as usual, but we'll get by. I'll have a gab with the old game warden. Seems like a decent kind. Might help us out."

Jim Cummins wasn't much help on that front, but I did find out why our reception had been so reserved.

"Brochet heard you was coming, couple of months ago. Schieff's manager spread the word you'd been up to some shady business – you and Charlie Schweder, when you canoed through here last summer. Said the Mounties was looking into it. You really pissed Isaac off when you bought your supplies for the rest of your trip from the Bay instead of from him. I'd like to help you and your pretty missus, but I got to stay neutral here . . . you understand?"

I thought to see what could be done for us by the Hudson's Bay Company but the manager was away on a journey to South End.

Winter was almost upon us, and we were without shelter and had no stocks of food or fuel. Moreover we felt more and more like interlopers in a tightly knit and unwelcoming community. Our prospects did not seem bright as we sought temporary shelter in a shack that was already occupied by a horde of red-backed mice. They, at least, welcomed us, acting as if we and our sleeping bags (especially our sleeping bags) were a gift from the gods.

We were rescued by Father Egenolf, big-nosed, white-haired, lean as a whippet, with a bony handshake that could have crushed a baseball. He came striding through our doorway one morning, his rust-coloured soutane hanging about his ankles, to tell us he had just returned from a distant fish camp where he had been netting a winter's supply of whitefish and lake trout for the three human and fifteen canine residents of his mission.

The Egg (as he was familiarly called, though never to his face) and I had met briefly during the summer of 1947. Now he gave me a tepid smile but lit up like a lantern as he grasped Fran's hand and kissed it with Gallic fervour.

"*Hélas!* Here is a *demoiselle* in distress, *non?* I shall rescue her!"

Soutane swirling, he led us to a log cabin belonging to a Cree family currently wintering at South End.

Eighteen feet square and one storey high, the cabin had one room and a tiny, windowless attic. The logs had been plastered with a yellowish mixture of mud and dry grass but most of this had fallen off, exposing numerous cracks and gaps. The tarpaper on the steeply pitched roof was in tatters and the panes in the three small windows cracked and grimy. The only furniture was a battered cast-iron cook-stove at the far end of a room floored with rough-hewn planks and ankle-deep in debris.

Father Egenolf arranged for us to rent this, the only unoccupied house in Brochet, for five dollars a month. The price was certainly right.

Having found a home for us, the Egg also provided a rusty, metal-framed bed, a lumpy mattress, and a splintered table. Then he gave us a month's supply of firewood. Despite being surrounded by the world's largest forest, firewood was precious stuff because most suitable trees within ten miles of Brochet had long since been consumed.

We still had to acquire a supply of basic food stuffs (flour, sugar, baking powder, oatmeal, bacon, and lard), together with everything else needed to keep us alive until spring. Neither of the trading posts had much to offer, most of their staples having already been purchased and carried off to camps and cabins on winter traplines. And Schieff's manager refused to let us have even a small portion of what remained in his store.

We had better luck at the Bay. Its manager – big, bluff British expatriate Bill Garbut – was initially wary of me but his elfin wife, Renée, immediately took to Fran. She loaned Fran priceless items of household equipment and winter clothing, while Bill gave me access to what remained of his post's stock and, at Renée's prodding, even provided scarce food supplies from their own private storeroom. Our acquisitions included fifty one-pound blocks of butter that had gone rancid and been "condemned" to be used as dog feed. I bought the lot, paying only a token sum, having discovered the rancidity was mainly restricted to the surface of the blocks, leaving the inner portion reasonably edible.

We spent the next few weeks furiously engaged in homemaking. Almost everything we needed was in short supply or non-existent, so we made do. Tools were few and primitive, yet we eventually put together a home that was not only comfortable but even stylish – by Brochet standards.

The smoke-grimed ceiling and dingy walls became resplendent with canary-yellow canoe enamel. I patched together cupboards, shelves, two chairs, and a kitchen counter from scraps of old packing cases, and Fran made curtains from the cheap but colourful cotton prints the Bay sold as women's dress goods. I sealed off the attic with layers of wrapping paper, converting it into a deep-freeze for caribou, fish, ptarmigan, rabbits, even a hind quarter of moose kindly sent our way by the game warden. I rolled several new layers of tarpaper over the roof and nailed saplings on top as protection from blizzards and winter gales. I caulked the log walls inside and out with strips of waste sacking and finally piled sand high against the foundation logs to keep out the worst winter drafts and all but the most persistent voles and mice.

Water and sanitation presented special problems. In summer every household supplied itself with water scooped by the pailful from the lake, and in winter from holes chopped through the lake ice, which froze to a thickness of several feet.

Toilets were non-existent, except in the traders' homes, some of which boasted chemical lavatories. The rest of us made do with vestigial outhouses sited anywhere from a dozen feet to a dozen yards from the cabins they served. Ours was a doorless, roofless construct with three skeletal walls and a horizontal pole bridging a shallow hole. It wasn't even really ours. Rather, it was a communal facility used by anybody and everybody living nearby. It was also a favourite hangout for some of Brochet's many stray and hungry dogs.

The prospect of my wife having to wait in line during a howling blizzard with the temperature at forty degrees below zero weighed heavily upon me. So I installed an empty ten-gallon lard pail in our attic that I made accessible by means of a trap door in the ceiling and a spruce-pole ladder. With the temperature well below zero, the attic was no place to linger: the cold up there quickly froze everything solid. Once a week I wrestled the icy pail down from its eyrie, rolled it outside and away from the house, then thawed it for an hour or more over an open fire so I could empty it.

The thawing of the bucket always drew an audience. A circle of ravenous dogs would form around me, drawing closer and closer until I drove them back with threatening gestures and shouts. A few human youngsters might also be present, watchful but, like the dogs, silent. They bestowed a descriptive name upon me – one still remembered when, twenty-six years later, I revisited Brochet in the company of Manitoba's then-premier, Edward Schreyer.

On that occasion a grinning Cree man amongst those gathered at the float dock to greet the dignitaries was heard to say, "So . . . Dog-soup Maker come back, eh? Wonder what he going to cook this time?"

Winter was in full swing before the first ski-equipped plane risked touching down on the ice at Brochet. It brought mail – including a stiff reprimand from my employer for having wasted my time and taxpayers' money the previous summer trying to ameliorate the desperate conditions of the Inuit I had encountered in southern Keewatin Territory. The letter concluded with these words:

"You are herewith instructed to refrain from meddling in matters outside your jurisdiction and to leave all such matters to competent authority."

To say I was upset by this would be to put it far too mildly. I railed against the ignorance and stupidity of the Ottawa mandarins, until Frances pulled me up.

"They probably *will* fire you if you carry on like this, though I don't suppose *that* will stop you. . . . Maybe you ought to quit this job now, then we could go back home where you could tell the papers what you've found out."

I had only recently been told by Father Egenolf's assistant of a mass grave for about forty Chipewyan men, women, and children who had perished in or near the settlement the previous spring of some unidentified disease. One that never *was* identified because the government doctor for the district was not able to find time to visit Brochet until a month after the lethal epidemic had run its course.

"We lose half our Idthen Eldeli [People of the Caribou] here and out at the camps," the young priest told me, smiling sadly. "*Eh bien.* They live like dogs, *les pauvres. Peut-être* it is better if the Lord takes them to His House for then they will be saved."

With these words sticking in my craw, I thought long and hard about what Fran had suggested. *Should* I tell my bosses in Ottawa to go to hell? And try writing something for the press about the abominable treatment of the native peoples I was seeing?

I had something else to think about as well. Having spent nearly five years as a sanctioned killer of my own kind, I was becoming increasingly averse to killing *any* living thing except to maintain the lives of me and mine. I was especially reluctant to slaughter caribou and wolves, as was required of me "in the interest of amassing scientific knowledge." But I was finding it hard to abandon the ambition I had nurtured since childhood of becoming a professional zoologist.

It was Hobson's choice, and the days slipped by without me making a decision.

Clock time had very little significance to those wintering in a community like Brochet. Our day began at dawn when, rousted by Tegpa's cold nose thrust into my face, I would scramble out of bed, rush to the cookstove, light the kindling I had carefully arranged the night before, then scoot back to the comfort of the double sleeping bag I shared with Fran to wait until the frigid cabin had warmed up at least to the freezing point.

When we could no longer see the frosty vapour of our breath, we would get up and, having broken the ice in the bucket, have a brief wash. Thereafter Fran would cook breakfast, usually cornmeal or oatmeal porridge with a slice or two of cold deer meat on the side, and our own homemade bread washed down by tea thickened and sweetened with evaporated milk.

As breakfast cooked, I would trot down to the lake armed with a twenty-pound iron bar flattened at one end in the form of a chisel, with which I would bash through the six or seven inches of new ice that had sealed our "well" during the night. Then, while Tegpa did his rounds, asserting and advertising his mastery over the local canines, I would shuttle five-gallon buckets of water back to the cabin.

Breakfast over, Fran would tackle her household chores, cooking, cleaning, mending our clothing, and doing the washing, while keeping the stove parsimoniously stoked with precious firewood, which was always in short supply. In the afternoons, weather permitting, she might snowshoe the half mile to the Bay for something she needed, or just to visit Renée. Or she might visit one of our closer neighbours, there to drink endless mugs of tea with the women and children while wrestling with the difficulty of trying to converse in a mixture of English, Cree, and Dene.

If the weather was reasonable (not more than thirty below and no blizzard blowing), I would strap on snowshoes and, accompanied by Tegpa, set off to check my trapline, which, to the bewilderment of the locals, consisted of fifty ordinary household *mouse* traps set under logs, tree stumps, or at inscrutable little holes in the snow. I did this because I was under instructions from my employer to "collect representative small mammals for taxonomic purposes and population analysis."

Tegpa and I regularly travelled ten or fifteen miles through frost-brittle Jack pine forest counting caribou and wolves (as much by their tracks as by their physical presence), and keeping a sharp lookout for ptarmigan or chicken (sharp-tailed grouse), which could be potted with a .22, *not* as specimens but to help fill our stomachs. Also I always carried a short axe in case we might come upon a stand of birch or tamarack previous generations had somehow overlooked.

I loved these excursions, as did Tegpa, and though we may not have learned a great deal about the specified "study species," we made the acquaintance of whisky-jacks (Canada jays), boreal chickadees, occasional ladder-backed woodpeckers, a porcupine, a great grey owl, and, on one truly momentous occasion, a wolverine, who looked us over challengingly from a few yards away until I unslung my .22, whereupon he pissed contemptuously in our direction before slogging off, belly deep in snow, with never a backward glance.

On occasion, I might join one of the local trappers in his carriole (a toboggan with built-up canvas sides, hauled by dogs) for a trip to a fish cache or trapping cabin as much as fifty miles away in the labyrinthine world of Reindeer Lake's boreal forest. On such excursions, I saw herds of caribou numbering as many as two or three hundred spending the daylight hours far out on the lake ice, where they could see would-be hunters, human or lupine, long before these could approach close enough to be a threat.

I had been instructed to "collect" up to a hundred caribou of all ages, together with as many wolves as I could shoot, trap, or poison, and had been provided with rifles, steel leghold traps, and cyanide bait for this purpose. I had been further instructed to dissect and minutely examine every specimen procured. External and internal parasites were to be identified, counted, and preserved in alcohol. The condition and state of development of sexual organs was to be ascertained, and a full range of foetuses preserved for future study. Stomach and bowel contents were to be analyzed – and so it went, ad nauseam.

I failed to comply.

Perhaps I refrained because of the growing conviction that studying animals alive in their own undisturbed habitat might reveal more truths about them than could be uncovered by gun and scalpel. I killed only one caribou during my time at Brochet, and it died not for Science but to provide food for the three of us. Moreover, I killed *no* wolves, nor did I make any attempt to do so.

During the long winter evenings Fran and I were often visited by neighbours, both white and native, or went visiting them. Few owned radios so conversation was the entertainment. They were exceptional storytellers, and even most of the youngsters had good tales to tell. After these visits, I would sometimes stay up past midnight, scribbling notes about travellers, hunters, missionaries, trappers, lovers, and losers; about Cree, Idthen Eldeli, Metis and whites, and the lives they led.

A bent toward writing was increasingly preoccupying me, and Fran's suggestion that I might have it in me to become a full-time writer seemed almost credible. I began spending a lot more time at my portable typewriter than in filling notebooks with scientific data as a dedicated biologist would have done. Of particular moment, I started expanding an account I had sketched earlier about the terrible events the year before that had decimated the Barren Land Inuit – especially the Ihalmiut of the Kazan River country.

By mid-November I had what I thought *might* be a publishable account of this disaster so, with Fran's encouragement and acting on the assumption that I might as well start at the top, I titled it *Eskimo Spring*, addressed it to the editor of the prestigious *Atlantic Monthly* magazine in Boston, USA, and sent it off with the next mail plane.

Then, feeling cocky at having perhaps loosened the fetters binding me to Ottawa, I decided to take a week off and travel by dog team to South End, a hundred and fifty miles away to see how the caribou, wolves, and people to the south were making out.

I borrowed a dog team and carriole from Shorty Laird, a white trapper temporarily laid up with a bad leg, and made ready to depart one crystalline morning with the mercury registering thirty below and just a breath of wind.

Shorty's eight dogs had been tied up for three weeks and were wild to run. It took me and two teenaged helpers half an hour to manhandle them into the harness, attaching them to the fifteen-foot-long carriole, which held my grub box, fifty pounds of frozen fish for dog feed, my sleeping bag and rifle, and a small packsack of odds and ends. I had tied the carriole to a stump while we harnessed the dogs, but somebody prematurely slipped the securing knot and, before I could jump aboard, the dogs were off like cannonballs. A fifty-foot brake rope was always towed behind the carriole in case of such emergencies, and I just managed to grab the free end as it whipped by and wrap it around one wrist, after which I was dragged through the settlement on my back at about thirty miles an hour.

Somehow I managed to swing myself around so I could use my feet as a brake. This got me nowhere and, once the dogs had dragged me onto the slick lake ice, there remained no further possibility of stopping or even slowing them. Nevertheless, I hung on for perhaps a quarter of a mile, while my arms felt as if they were being wrenched from their sockets; then I let go.

I got shakily to my feet as carriole and dogs grew small in the distance. Looking back, I could see a small troop of neighbours ranged along the shore, motionless as gargoyles but undoubtedly enjoying to the full the spectacular discomfiture of the tenderfoot.

As I limped grimly back to make arrangements for a search team to pursue the runaways, I knew I had secured a permanent place in Brochet's panoply of stories.

The cold intensified as December settled in, and the mud chinking of our cabin could not keep it out. Although the indoor temperature at waist level remained tolerable, water spilled on the floor froze almost immediately.

Slipping on a patch of this instant ice brought me inspiration. I began saving our waste water, which I then heated in galvanized pails on the back of the stove. When I had a couple of full pails ready, I would carry them outside, add as much snow as possible, then slather this slush on the outer walls of the house, where it froze instantly. When our cabin was ice-sheathed up to the level of the ceiling, it became much more liveable. Soon almost every cabin in Brochet acquired similar igloo-like armour and my stock went up a little.

In mid-December a small bush plane belonging to one of Isaac Schieff's many interlocking little companies slithered to a halt on the ice of Brochet Bay to unload freight for his trading post, together with some mail.

There were letters for both Fran and me – not all bearing good news. A stiffly worded epistle from the University of Toronto informed me that my college had decided not to let me complete my current year extramurally – an arrangement that had been agreed upon before I went north in the spring of 1947. I was on notice that if I wanted a degree I would have to resume classes in Toronto by mid-January of the coming year.

Fran was outraged by what we both felt was a low blow, but I had mixed feelings. I had always known that a career in science would require me to obtain a bachelor's degree, then a master's, and finally a doctorate, but this academic climb to success had never had any attraction for me. Now I was tempted to use this setback as an excuse for abandoning academe altogether and becoming an unfettered "naturalist" able – perhaps – to make a living studying the wild ones alive and *in* the wild. I might have done it then and there had not Frances been dubious.

Schieff's plane's principal cargo was liquor, and most of the customers celebrated fiercely over the next several days and nights, turning Brochet into Bedlam. Guns blasted salutes at all hours – and not all were aimed at nothing. To Father Egenolf's helpless fury, several bullet holes appeared in the steeple of his new church.

Fights erupted between employees and adherents of the Bay and of Schieff's company. Combatants included white and Metis trappers, together with drifters from a commercial fishing venture Schieff had started. The hullabaloo was enough to put the caribou and wolf populations to flight and even to persuade many of the resident ravens to seek safety in the woods.

One night, when the temperature had sunk to forty-five below zero, two Metis men failed to find their way home after a bash at Schieff's and froze to death. I thought it a wonder more did not meet a similar fate. Indeed, Fran and I thawed out and resuscitated one unfortunate who, wearing little more than a flannel shirt and torn trousers, passed out in a snowdrift near our cabin. Had Tegpa not drawn our attention to him, he might never have awakened.

Our concern about what was going on was not shared by others. When I spoke about it to Jim Cummins, the game warden, who was also the magistrate, he offered this nonchalant advice.

"Don't let it bother you. If people gets enough liquor into them they'll stay warm even if hell freezes over. Anyhow, this lot of booze'll run out soon enough, then they'll quiet down."

Binge drinking and wild parties were not the worst of it. Fran was unnerved and I was infuriated by the hostility unleashed by some "under-the-influence" white residents. One evening Schieff's manager (whom I will call Belson) barged into our home to announce belligerently that he had come for Tegpa, whom he fancied as a new leader of his dog team and had already several times tried to buy. I had always refused, so now he tried a different tack.

"Your goddamn husky's been into my fish shed stuffing his gut. Either you pay me twenty-five bucks for the fish he stole *and* turn him over to me for my team . . . or I'll shoot the fucker dead first chance I get."

He then stamped out of the cabin, sweeping Fran's china teapot (a precious loan from Renée Garbut) off the kitchen counter, shattering it into tiny fragments. When I told the usually affable Bill Garbut about this incident, his benevolent expression hardened into a scowl.

"That son of a bitch would shoot his own mother for the fun of it. The way he screws the natives – and it's more ways than one – makes me puke. . . . Let me tell you a little story about him.

"There used to be a Chip kid here with a wizened-up arm from polio he got when he was a baby. He had epilepsy too – took fits. He wasn't too smart but he always tried to do his best. His family was part of the Hatchet Lake band but Nazee – that was his name – couldn't make it out on the land with the rest of them so the mission was supposed to be looking after him.

"He got by, running errands and doing odd jobs nobody else would do. A lot of them for Belson, who paid the kid with spoiled stuff from his store nobody would buy.

"Winter evenings, Belson and his cronies – white trappers and the like – would amuse themselves giving Nazee lemon extract and when he was tipsy – the stuff's three-quarters alcohol – make him strip to the buff and dance round a red-hot pot-belly stove. Crippled like he was, he would sometimes fall against the stove.

"Then they'd give him some more extract, and get out the marking hammer.

"You know what that is, don't you? Hammer with sharp little nails set into its head, used to bash a fox skin or any fur to make a pattern into it. Kind of a trademark that shows the skin belongs to your outfit.

"Those bastards would pay Nazee with shots of extract, or some-times a nickel or even a dime, to let them bash *him* with Schieff's hammer. Mostly they'd do it on his backside, but sometimes on his crippled arm or his legs, under his clothes where it wouldn't show.

"When I got wind of that, I sent for the boy and when Renée and I saw the brand hammered into that wizened arm I sent a message down to Belson offering to shoot *him* if he done it again. When I told Egenolf about it, he just shrugged and said it was in God's hands. The sanctimonious old bugger! I sure and hell knew whose hands that kid was in, and it wasn't God's!

"Renée wanted us to keep the kid around but I couldn't do that because Company policy don't run to charity. Anyhow, the kid went someplace else. Don't know where. But that bastard Belson's still around! I keep hoping somebody'll fill him full of lead."

During this drunken period, the native people kept a low profile and some withdrew to their bush camps. They even stayed clear of Fran and me. I wondered why, but concluded they probably thought we whites were all alike. Perhaps we gave them occasion to think so. After the Garbuts threw a party to celebrate the first anniversary of our marriage, I wrote in my journal:

> *The main refreshment was punch made of about a quart of grain alcohol from my scientific supplies, a couple of bottles of Vat 69 out of Bill's private stock, a lot of Renée's homemade beer, some cans of grapefruit segments, a bottle of maple syrup, some mouldy lemons, and a good big dollop of cayenne pepper. After a few mugs of this Bill was reborn as an Apache and danced wildly about to music he made himself – the mating call of a bull moose.*
>
> *Some Crees just in from South End with fur to trade found the post door locked and our lot whooping it up inside. They stood outside the frosted windows peering in at the antics of the "master race." Wonder what they thought of it all. Don't think I'll ask.*

Jim Cummins had been right about one thing: when the planeload of liquor was gone, Brochet quieted down. Hardly a soul was to be seen outdoors during the brief daylight hours and at night even the occupied cabins seemed to belong to an abandoned settlement. Almost the only sign of life was underfed dogs drifting about like disembodied spirits.

The next plane to arrive was a Norseman chartered by the federal Department of Indian Affairs. It brought in a Dr. Robert Yule on the last of four visits scheduled for 1948 to provide for the medical requirements of the natives who lived at or traded to Brochet. Amiable, middle-aged Dr. Yule might have chosen a better time to perform his duties. On the day he arrived, there were fewer than twenty natives in the settlement – the rest being far away at winter camps or on their traplines. Had the good doctor chosen to delay his visit until the Christmas season, the entire population of the region would have been gathered here. He and his plane stayed with us exactly twenty-five minutes – Bill Garbut timed it – while the doctor saw (but did not treat) a Dene youth with a broken leg that had already begun to set crookedly, and several elderly people to whom he handed out large white pills he carried loose in his pocket. They looked like after-dinner mints but Bill claimed they were laxatives. Then he gave us all a smiling farewell and flew back to his home in The Pas.

His departure left me seething, for he had been responsible for the health of the natives of the region during the fearful epidemic in the spring of 1947 when at least two hundred men, women, and children – an accurate count was never made – perished of a disease that was never diagnosed because no doctor visited any of the afflicted camps. But *I* had visited several of them while making the canoe journey between Reindeer and Nueltin Lakes four months after the dying and had seen many of the hurriedly made graves which now housed the inhabitants of those otherwise-deserted sites.

The memory of those graves and the mass grave Father Darveaux had told me about impelled me to write a report about the abominable way the natives of this region were being treated. I detailed the government's failure to provide medical aid or help of *any* sort during the 1947 epidemic and concluded my tirade with a bald account of the treatment the crippled boy, Nazee, had received.

Before sending my outburst to my superiors in Ottawa, I showed it to Bill Garbut. He said little, other than to ask my permission to make a copy of the Nazee story. I was not surprised when, a few days later, he told me he had arranged to have the copy mailed anonymously from Winnipeg to Isaac Schieff.

"That money-grubbing old bugger hired Belson after the Bay fired him for frigging with the mail. Schieff knew he was no damn good. Maybe this'll give him some second thoughts. He's scared shitless of the press."

Within a week, the moccasin telegraph was spreading the news that Belson was being replaced by Schieff's son as manager at Brochet.

By mid-December, with Christmas fast approaching, Brochet was filling up.

> *One by one the empty cabins are sprouting smoke from their tin chimneys as the human and dog population swells. It's a rather mysterious phenomenon because they all seem to arrive in the middle of the night. You wake up in the morning and there they are! Tents are going up too, which means the Barren Land Chips have begun to arrive all the way from Nueltin Lake. The traders are busier than beavers. Lots of activity and lots of chicanery as furs are swapped for gewgaws, gadgets, and sometimes even useful stuff like food and ammunition.*

A week later I wrote:

> *The settlement is overflowing with a couple of hundred adults and at least sixty children. The trading posts are jam-packed from morning until night. Brochet Bay looks like a dog rodeo, with teams racing over it every direction and sled tracks as thick as threads in a white handkerchief. The mission is doing a roaring business too, collecting furs for tithes, hearing confessions, selling pardons, and, I wouldn't doubt, indulgences.*

*Although it's running mostly on tea now instead of booze, which has pretty well run out, the social life never seems to stop. Candles and oil lanterns burn all night in every cabin and the natives, most of whom haven't seen each other for a couple of months, just never seem to get enough visiting. Dog teams are as thick as taxis in New York and cries of "Hew" and "Haw" (left and right) sound like a hassle of mad ravens. The teams compete for right of way and there are glorious free-for-all dog fights with lots of cursing in Cree, Chip, English, and canine. When we go walkabout we carry good thick sticks to keep the dog mob at bay. At night there is a deafening cacophony from two or three hundred hungry dogs each wanting another chunk of whitefish or caribou. Little mountains of crushed bones, fish scales, deer hair, and dog shit grow like mushrooms around every dog tethering post. Things were actually quieter around here when the booze was on the go.*

*Christmas is the main celebration of the year because winter dog travel makes it possible for almost everyone – men, women, young-sters, and old folks – to come to Brochet even from the most distant camps. But though most of the natives are nominally Christians – Catholics – neither religion nor trade is the principal draw. The big attraction is human companionship: the need and opportunity to renew the sense of belonging to a family, clan, or tribe.*

*Christmas becomes the time, and Brochet the place for far-flung and wandering people to see and touch one another; a time for young guys and gals to make out, with marriage often the outcome; a time and place for old folk to circulate and pass on the knowledge they've acquired; a time for storytelling, dances, "socials." A time and place for the renewal and repair of the human fabric.*

*There is something else as well.*

*This annual get-together is almost certainly fuelled by an ancient, maybe instinctive, need to renew the allegiance that not only binds human beings to one another, but cements all living things into the single, super-entity that constitutes life on earth.*

*These people are doing what their pagan ancestors (and ours too) used to do every year at the time of the winter solstice: they are refurbishing and strengthening their essential connections to the mother-with-a-thousand-names who is the mother of us all.*

*For nearly two thousand years Christianity has been trying to make over this celebration, and refashion it into a weapon we can use in our ongoing war to subjugate all the world and (madmen's dream!) even the universe, to serve our boundless ambitions and insatiable desires.*

*This isn't the kind of dream my native neighbours seem to have. I believe they'd be content with what they had, with their old ways and old beliefs – if only we'd let them.*

Nineteen forty-nine was almost upon us, but Frances and I had not yet decided what course to steer.

One morning while I was out on the bay chipping at nearly a foot of new ice that had formed in our well overnight, I saw the corporal from the weather station knocking on the door of our cabin. He had brought us a radiogram. By the time I got back with the water, he was gone but Fran wordlessly handed me the flimsy. Unlike most government communications, this one was concise and to the point.

AS OF DECEMBER THIRTY ONE YOUR SERVICES HAVE BEEN
DEEMED REDUNDANT
   R A GIBSON
DEPUTY COMMISSIONER NORTHWEST TERRITORIES OF
CANADA AND DEPUTY MINISTER DEPARTMENT OF MINES
AND RESOURCES CANADA

"Looks like they got my report," I said a little ruefully.
Fran was half smiling, half crying. "Well, what now?"

"As if you didn't know," I said and kissed her. "Goodbye, Brushy . . . Hello Toronto. Hope Tegpa can handle it!"

Our removal was neither quickly nor easily arranged. Pulling up the rootlets we had established and packing our few belongings did not take long, but finding a plane to take us out was more demanding. The Schieff Norseman seemed the obvious answer, but the post's new manager equivocated until it was obvious we were never going to be flown out by his company's plane. Eventually I arranged for a charter from Flin Flon, but a week of fierce storms intervened before a plane could pick us up.

> *January 5th. Lovely day, clear, bright, and, thank God, no wind. We're bunking in with the Garbuts while we wait, but this morning we walked back to the cabin to say goodbye. Bit of a heart-breaker, those tacky chintz curtains, the egg-yellow walls with the bare spots where we had pinned up pictures cut from old magazines, all the stuff we made and did to help the old place turn itself into a home. Now all of a sudden it's empty as a biscuit tin. I hope the Moiestie family comes back and lives in it again. It won't last long without people.* *

---

* When I revisited Brochet in 1974, the house was still standing. It was the last log building still in use, all the others having been replaced with prefabricated plywood boxes. A young Cree couple was camping in it until they, too, could acquire a modern box.

# › 2 ›

## FAR FROM THE
## MADDING CROWD

An old Fairchild bush plane with cracked skis and fabric-patched wings finally carried us south from Brochet. Fran rode up front with a sleepy young pilot while Tegpa and I scrunched into a narrow space atop our belongings in the freezing kennel of a cabin. The old plane shook like a jelly and its unmuffled engine roared and brayed as if in agony. But all went well, and a few hours later we landed at Flin Flon, where we boarded a train for Winnipeg. From Winnipeg the trans-Canada express took us to Toronto's Union Station to be welcomed by Reuben Thornhill, Frances's father. He drove us to the Thornhill home, where we were to stay until we got settled.

Rube was a hardware salesman who had weathered the Depression while still managing to buy the cramped, semi-detached house in which he and his wife, Florence, had raised their daughter. Frances, Tegpa, and I were given the third floor – two tiny attic rooms in one of which was a sink and a hot plate. We were delighted to share the family bathroom on the second floor, which was equipped with a toilet that did not need to be emptied outside every week. *And* there was a bathtub in which we could luxuriate as long as we pleased.

Fran and I were comfortable, but Tegpa, who had lived most of his young life in a world without constraints, probably found it the equivalent of a maximum-security prison. After three days of train travel chained to the wall of a baggage car, he had arrived in Toronto to find himself confined to a small box within a box and not even permitted to range around the bleak little backyard except while tethered to a clothesline. This was necessary to keep him from being run over, for he had no experience with motor vehicles.

Life grew even harder for him. His thick, heavy coat was too warm in these urban, southern conditions and in consequence he developed a raging rash that spread across his body like fire. When I took him to the Secord Clinic, reputedly the best animal hospital in Toronto, I was given a tube of ointment, and the veterinarian admonished me for having exposed my dog to unhygienic conditions during the rail journey south.

Tegpa was in such discomfort, bordering I think on agony, that he could not sleep in the heat of the house, so we made a bed for him in the unheated porch, where I spread my sleeping bag on an old mattress to keep him company.

It was not enough.

One morning near the end of January, I woke from fitful sleep, reached over to touch his muzzle and so reassure both him and me – and got no response.

Tegpa was gone.

And so one of the few living threads in the fragile tie with which I had been trying to connect myself for two years to the world from which he came was severed.

———

Two days after our return to Toronto I was back at university.

Within a week I was finding it insufferable. Why, I wondered, had I voluntarily submitted myself to this confinement in the company of a mob of strangers, most of whom were several years my junior, who knew nothing of life and death in faraway places, and who shared few if any of my admittedly hazy hopes and expectations. They were not of my tribe nor I of theirs, and by the end of the month I was ready to abandon university; which I might well have done had it not been that a few professors allowed me what almost amounted to carte blanche in topics and writing style for my term essays. The hours I spent at my battered old typewriter in the attic apartment of my parents-in-law's Toronto house made the early months of 1950 endurable, if barely so.

In due course I was granted a pass Bachelor of Arts degree – but did not attend the graduation ceremony. I had more pressing things to do. Late in January I had received a reply to the letter I had sent *Atlantic* magazine from Brochet. The reply – written by the assistant to Dudley Cloud, editor of the Atlantic Monthly Press – informed me that Cloud had "found it interesting and would be glad to hear more from Mr. Mowat about his writing plans."

Interpreting this cautious letter as an open sesame to the world of literary wonders, I had replied to the effect that I had a book in mind about the fascinating native people of Keewatin and, as soon as my university work allowed, would send Mr. Cloud an outline. I begged him to bear with me.

Although during the subsequent three months I heard nothing further from Boston, the idea of a book about the Ihalmiut had developed a life of its own and I was anxious to bring it to birth. But where, and how?

I had had more than my fill of the city. The prospect of being trapped in its stinking canyons through the long summer months was more than I could face.

My father wanted me to accept a job with the publishing house of Macmillan Canada, but the idea of bedding down in Toronto stood my back hairs on end.

What I really wanted was to return to the north, but without means or backing this was an extremely tenuous possibility. Furthermore, Fran was adamant that if I chose to go back north I would go alone.

Our plans seemed to have stalled until one day we met Elford Cox, a teacher and sometime sculptor at Upper Canada College who had recently bought a farm in the Albion Hills some forty miles northwest of Toronto.

"Mostly swamps and sandhills. Not a lot of wilderness, but pretty private for being only an hour from the city. There's way more land than I need so I could let you have a chunk."

The weather was fine and springlike when Fran and I drove out to have a look at El's farm. It lay on a great glacial moraine strewn with sand-and-gravel hillocks and swampy valleys. It was also strewn with the abandoned farms of nineteenth-century Irish immigrants who had scrabbled a living from it through three generations but who had so impoverished the thin soil that the land was worn out. The farmers had mostly fled but earlier inhabitants, including deer, foxes, porcupines, mink, even beavers, were returning as new stands of conifers and hardwoods began reclaiming the desolation.

This incipient renewal of life struck a chord with me, and I concluded the Albion Hills might be a place where I could live for a while. Fran was enthusiastic, viewing it as an acceptable compromise between the north and the city.

"We could have a little place of our own here and be as private as you like. With birds and beasts galore. You'd be close to publishers and to magazines you could write for."

I was not so sure. The north was pulling hard and, although I had heard nothing further from Boston, I nurtured hopes of Atlantic Press taking my proposed book and offering me an advance that would cover the costs of a return to the Ihalmiut country, if only for a season.

But time and my small savings were running out. When Cox offered to "let me have" a piece of his farm for a "nominal" sum, I succumbed and so, for five hundred dollars, Fran and I became the owners of ten acres of wooded swamp and a bald-headed hill. There was no building, but I concluded that if we concentrated on construction through the summer season, we could have a roof over our heads before snow fell.

On May 10 of 1949, Fran and I drove Lulu Belle (a civilian version of the military jeeps I had driven during the war) to the site of our future home. Pavement took us west out of Toronto past Woodbridge, where a gravel-surfaced road continued north to Bolton, a farming community of about five hundred people destined to be our closest "urban" centre. Ten miles beyond Bolton we passed through the decaying village of Palgrave and a few miles farther on turned west on the 30th side road of Albion Township.

The 30th was a road only by courtesy. Originally built for foot travellers, wagons, and sleighs, it was now an obstacle course. In winter it was often clogged with snow. In spring it became a sequence of mud wallows linked by pretty little stretches of standing water where wood ducks happily swam. In summer the 30th was nominally passable for motor vehicles, but so pitted and rutted that even farm tractors sometimes "bottomed out."

Two weeks of exceptionally fine weather in early May had worked wonders on it, but even with four-wheel drive Lulu Belle needed an hour to worry her way the few miles westward to where a break in a decrepit split-cedar fence suggested an entrance to our little Eden.

The simile seems apt because we had not driven a hundred feet along the base of our naked hill when we encountered a metre-long fox snake resplendent in rich chocolate chevrons and golden scales.

Having only recently exchanged its winter skin for a glistening new one, it was too preoccupied to pay us much heed. I gave it the right of way while Fran curled her feet up under her (the jeep had no doors). We waited in the warm spring sunshine until the snake had eased itself into the tall grass, then we got out and set about deciding just where we should build our house.

What we were going to build had already been decided. Fran's original preference had been for a two-storey house of modern design. Mine had been for a back-country cabin a little larger and more elaborate than our Brochet home had been. Fran had visions of permanence, but I had no desire to put down roots just yet. Furthermore, I only had about a thousand dollars, which would have to put a roof over our heads and also sustain us through the next several months while we built our home with our own hands.

Fran accepted a compromise design – a three-room, 20-by-30-foot log house with a 20-by-15-foot cellar under one end of it. I had hoped to cut the logs from trees growing on our own property but there were not nearly enough of sufficient girth. This stymied me until I heard about a newborn company offering construction logs at a price even I could afford. The upstart Air-Lock Log Company's product was cheap because the logs were actually industrial waste – the cores of birch logs that had been peeled down to a uniform diameter of six inches to produce thin sheets of veneer from which plywood had been manufactured. At a total cost of $404.60, delivered, these logs were the answer to a poor man's prayer. Ours were scheduled for delivery in the later part of May, which meant we would have to hustle to prepare a foundation for them.

To keep us until we had our house built, we had a borrowed tent under a clump of spruce trees, with an outdoor fireplace, and a table and a couple of benches knocked up from scrap lumber.

Two days after we had set up camp, a dump truck backed onto our property and tipped out a huge pile of naked yellow logs. It took

Fran and me a full day to sort out this pile of giant pick-up sticks and stack them so they would not warp out of shape under the summer sun.

Then we got down to work.

My tool kit was not much different from those of the first homesteaders in Albion Township. I had an axe, round-mouthed shovel, spade, pickaxe, sledgehammer, crosscut saw, and a kit of smaller carpentry tools. I had *no* power tools, not even a chainsaw, and no access to any source of power except our muscles and Lulu Belle.

The first major job was digging out the cellar. When outlined on the ground with sticks and string, it did not look as if it would be a very formidable problem, but once the sod had been stripped away and its third dimension laid bare, I found myself facing a Herculean task. I set to with pick and shovel, heaving the dirt into a wooden "dump box" I had built into Lulu Belle's after-end. About a hundred shovelfuls were needed to fill this box, by which time I was very glad to get behind the steering wheel and bounce slowly across our hill to a ravine where I could dump the spoil.

Unloading was fun. Having backed Lulu to the lip of the ravine, I would hook one end of a logging chain to the box and the other to a stout old maple tree on the far side of the hollow. Then I would put Lulu into bull-low gear and four-wheel drive and inch her ahead until the box was pulled out of her rear compartment to spill its contents into the ravine.

As the cellar hole deepened, it became increasingly difficult to fling the dirt up into the box. By the time I had dug three feet down, I could no longer manage. The solution was to cut a ramp into the cellar wall and back Lulu down it. As the cellar grew deeper, the ramp had to be deepened and lengthened. Digging the cellar and the ramp required the removal of at least eighty tons of earth from a hole that, had it been filled with water, would have made a good-sized swimming pool.

———

Spring came and went. The world around us flowered, and a multitude of birds sang, made love, and reared their young. But I was hardly aware of anything except the gaping pit into which Lulu every day backed a little farther, and I sank a little deeper.

Fran was game to help with the excavation but it required more strength than she had. So she kept "house," got the meals, washed the few bits of clothing I bothered to wear, kept me supplied with tea or lemonade so I wouldn't become completely dehydrated, and generally fetched and carried. When I could spare Lulu, Fran drove to Palgrave for the mail but mostly to hear another human voice (it belonged to our gossip of a postmistress, who also kept the village store). Occasionally Fran drove as far afield as Bolton, in search of essentials. Luxuries, such as beer and booze, were not to be had nearer than Toronto, except from bootleggers at prices we could not afford.

By mid-June, the pit was about five feet deep, and I was sweating in this hole one day when a visitor came calling. A potato farmer from a long lineage of potato farmers, he was one of those whose land had become so impoverished it would no longer feed him and his family so he was now moonlighting as Albion Township's tax assessor. A scarecrow with a vacant stare, he did not introduce himself but silently regarded me and my excavation long enough to make me feel uneasy. Then he spat a gob of tobacco juice into the pit and in measured tones barely above the level of a whisper, told me, "Cain't dig no grave on private property. 'Tain't allowed. Them as is gone has got to go into the churchyard."

I was amused at what I took to be a sally of local wit. I was less amused when, some months later, I got my first tax bill. It was for a sum about three times higher than that for any comparative property in Albion. The last laugh was surely his.

When the digging was finished, I became a mason. To assist me in providing concrete footings for the cellar walls, the fireplace, and the foundation pillars, Lulu metamorphosed into a combined sand, gravel, and cement truck. Her rated carrying capacity was only 500 pounds, but she fetched much heavier loads of pit-run gravel from a farmer's field three miles away, small mountains of bagged cement from Bolton, and 45-gallon drums (two at a time) of water scooped with a pail from a small stream running beneath a nearby concession road.

I had no motor-driven mixer so I cobbled a mixing trough from ancient planks taken from an abandoned barn. The machinery was me, a shovel, and a hoe. I carried the resultant slurry to where it was needed in a wheelbarrow or in twin buckets slung from a neck yoke.

One torrid July morning the unusual sound of a car climbing our hill gave me an excuse to take a break. I returned to camp half-naked, sweat-soaked and filmed with cement dust, to find Frances in animated conversation with a dark-haired youngish woman sporting the insignia of the Women's Royal Canadian Naval Service (the WRNS) in which Fran had served during the war.

Both seemed perturbed in my presence. In a low voice, Fran identified the stranger as having once been her Commanding Officer, but offered no explanation as to why this officer had tracked down a lowly "ranker" such as Fran had been.

The visitor was distinctly ill at ease, and when I suggested she might like to take potluck lunch with us, she hurriedly declined.

I had to leave them at that point for I had a mix of concrete on the go. When I returned to camp an hour later, the visitor was gone. Frances was sobbing in the tent and would not come out or talk to me.

She remained withdrawn and unreachable for several days. Then one evening she drove into Palgrave, where there was a public telephone. When she returned, she announced that she had decided to return to her parents and stay with them while taking a summer course toward the degree she had abandoned when we got married. I was gob-smacked, as Newfoundlanders say. I felt guilty now at having cut short her university career, although at the time I had assumed *she* wanted to escape from the university as much as I did.

Next day I drove her to the city and left her at her parents' home. We parted amicably, though almost as strangers. Neither of us could, or would, scale the wall that had so suddenly risen between us.

We saw very little of one another during much of the rest of the summer, although I did make three or four visits to the Thornhill home and on one occasion Fran's parents brought her to our building site for a brief and uncomfortable visit. It was not a success. All four of us seemed enmeshed in a conspiracy of silence. Looking back on that summer now, I view the entire sorry contretemps as scenes from a confusing silent movie bereft even of explanatory subtitles. And so it must remain.

That summer was viciously hot. One August day the heat became so intolerable I abandoned my labours and fled to a swimming hole on a nearby tributary of the Humber River.

The pool was barely large enough for me and a school of small minnows called rainbow dace, but we shared it anyway. As they inquisitively nibbled at my bare skin, I downed several warm beers and tried to relax but I was too troubled for that. I could not – *would not* – accept the likelihood that my marriage had come unstuck and, worse still, that it might be *my own fault*. I felt guilty, and was angry about that. I was enormously frustrated, almost incapacitated, and helpless to rectify the situation.

Angrily flinging an empty beer bottle into the woods, and sending the dace fleeing in all directions, I stumbled out of the pond and went back to work. There was solace – of a sort – to be found in working my ass off, and I could see no other way to fill the void.

When the house foundation was more or less completed, it was time to put on a carpenter's hat. I was a rank amateur at that trade, but the gods were kind. Late in July two ex-soldiers bought the abandoned farm directly to the south. Lloyd Coombs and Ben Green were of my own age and both had been carpenters before the war. Having purchased a war-surplus army truck, an old tractor, and a newfangled chainsaw, they were setting themselves up as lumbermen-builders. Since we were all "vets," we became friends and they were of great assistance to me in the days that followed. They gave me expert advice and were almost my only human contacts until early in September, when Fran's parents brought her back to me.

She and I were smilingly polite to each other, but nothing was said about the shadowed weeks just passed. Those weeks never did reveal their secrets to me, remaining a disturbing and unsolved mystery to this day.

Shortly after Fran's return, we began raising the log walls of our house. She made herself useful, uncomplainingly rolling logs to the site; holding them firm while I sawed and drilled; and, as the walls slowly rose, keeping me supplied with caulking cotton and the ten-inch nails that pinned the logs together. The blight upon our marriage seemed to dissipate through this shared labour. We became comrades – then lovers once again. Although it was evident we would have to work like the very devil if we were to have a roof over our heads before snow fell I began to feel we might actually pull it off.

We had little social life that autumn. Our few neighbours were generally a dour lot who may well have thought us unhinged for trying to establish ourselves in the wasteland they and their forebears had created. Relatives occasionally visited. One sultry day my father drove in, not to offer any physical or financial assistance but to deliver a homily. It was high time, he said, for me (and Frances too, if she wished) to enrol in the University of Toronto's Library School. From there we could expect to graduate into useful and rewarding careers, as he and my mother had done after the First World War. His advice was well meant so I did not take it amiss. I did, however, resent his parting shot that day, addressed to Fran.

"I should have warned you before that Farley is the roughest carpenter ever conceived. If two planks come within an inch of each other, he considers it a tight fit. I hope your cabin will hold together without too much putty."

Raising the walls had been slow, tedious work. The roof went on more quickly, and by the end of September only two major tasks remained – water, and sewage disposal.

For the well I chose a site close to the house and began digging. At twelve feet, the bottom of my shaft was still bone dry and I was ready to call it quits. Each bucket of earth had to be hauled to the surface with a block and tackle hung from a wooden tripod with the loaded bucket swinging ponderously over me all the while. It was a singularly happy day when water began bubbling up beneath my feet and sent me scrambling up the rickety ladder. But there was no time to celebrate. The water was rising fast and, without cribbing, the surrounding earth would soon begin to slump into what would certainly become a huge and muddy crater. Lloyd, Ben, and I quickly manhandled into place the cylindrical wooden crib I had built and slid it down the hole. We didn't have *running* water but it was water that could at least be carried into the house as needed.

For the toilet, I dug another pit over which I erected a sturdy privy made of freshly milled, sweet-smelling cedar. I lovingly crafted the seat from a piece of splinter-proof maple, sandpapered until it was, as Lloyd admiringly put it, "smooth as a baby's bum." As was the custom, I cut a crescent moon through the door so the occupant could see out and give warning of prior possession to other customers.

Some years later my privy gained fame of a sort when Pierre Berton, then a columnist for the *Toronto Star*, revealed that I had found some discarded store dummies and rescued two nude female half-models which were more or less intact but in need of tender loving care.

*Farley took them home to Frances but she absolutely refused to give them house room so he set them up in his backhouse, where they became permanent residents. They sat, one on each side of the throne, and were the cynosure of all eyes – including mine.*

On September 13 I finished hanging the front door of a house that was basically an empty shell. There were three rooms: the kitchen-cum-bedroom; an even smaller one earmarked as a bathroom if and when we got running water but which meanwhile served as a carpentry shop; and a relatively spacious room, eighteen by twenty feet, dominated by the huge fireplace. This *was* truly our living room. We ate there; read there; listened to music on a tinny little battery radio; and, in one corner, I tried to write.

There was no electricity, no telephone, and no furnace. Though the fireplace provided more than enough heat, it consumed wood like a Mississippi steamboat. The kitchen boasted our only luxuries: a refrigerator that, improbably, kept things cool by burning propane gas, and a propane-fuelled cookstove. A great deal of work remained to be done, inside and out – but not just yet. We had run out of money so it was necessary for me to switch hats again. I dusted off my battered typewriter and tried to reconnect with Dudley Cloud, to whom I had last written in May and from whom I had heard nothing since.

*October 17, 1949*

*Dear Mr. Cloud:*

*This day a fire burns in the fireplace of our new home and we have a half-bottle of inferior rum with which to celebrate the end of our servitude to the Great Brown Beast – the house. It is finished – well, partly – and it only remains to pay for it.*

*I won't bother you with excuses for my long silence and apparent failure to act on your request for an outline of my Eskimo book. . . . I have thought long and hard about it and now have time to put those thoughts on* paper. I also have the stimulus – financial – and it is pressing. I will have an outline in the mail by the end of the month but I must warn you, in order to support bodies and souls I will quickly have to produce potboilers for magazines, but will not allow them to interfere with the main chance.

I have recently had word about the Ihalmiut. A polio epidemic that swept the eastern arctic this summer has, for all practical purposes, written finis to their history as a coherent group. The handful of survivors will probably be transplanted to the coast, where they will merge with the so-called civilized Eskimos. It will not be many years before these people of the deer are quite forgotten. I wish to God I could have had ten years with them.

My book about them could be in the form of a story, a sort of "profile" based on the life of Pommela, the old man who has been their chief shaman – sorcerer – during their final years. The central theme would concern itself with the impact of the white race on this man, on his people, and so on all of the Eskimoan people. . . .

My wife has instructed me to thank you for the copy of M. De Poncin's book Eskimos that caught up with us last month after long wanderings about the arctic pursuing me. The book doesn't seem to have gained anything in authenticity from its travels, but I am instructed to thank you and, being an obedient husband, do so. But what purpose did you intend for this book? Its pages are far too hard and shiny to have any practical value in our sylvan retreat.

Cheerio for now. I hope you will bear with me a while longer. Life for those who defy the Big Machine can be damned difficult and the Mowats have had a hard summer.

Two weeks later I wrote again, this time enclosing a 2,100-word book outline.

I have had second thoughts about the Pommela story. If, instead of using Pommela's life as the central theme, I expand it to include the

*Ihalmiut as a whole, it should make it easier to tie in a number of related subjects. Three of these – biology, anthropology, and geography – have been major interests of mine for many years. Biology led me to study the Barrenland Caribou and the Arctic Wolf together with many other animals of the region. To give you an idea of what I've been doing in this connection, let me tell you briefly about the wolf work.*

*In May of 1947 I located a wolf den not too far from our camp and for the next six weeks spent much of my time in a small tent near the den spying and prying into the family life of the more or less unsuspecting wolves through a 15x binocular telescope. This resulted in my acquiring much scientific data, and even more illuminating and thought-provoking observations that I think are both amusing and enlightening. This study concluded with a visit to the den, down which I crawled under the mistaken belief there were no wolves at home. But there were. Three of them, in fact.*

*My anthropological studies included the folklore, religion, hunting methods, etc. etc. of the Ihalmiut: an archaeological survey of their portion of the central Barrenlands of Keewatin and, most important of all, personal relationships with many of the surviving Ihalmiut. I have been able to build up a fairly good idea of what the aboriginal culture was like and to recon- struct at least some of their history during the last half century and more.*

*I also spent some months in the country of the Idthen Eldeli, the most northerly Indian people of the region, and have enough material about them to begin a book but would dearly love to spend more time with them.*

*White men also provide a splendid source of material ranging from the story of mad "Eskimo" Charlie, to the 45-year sojourn of a German missionary priest on the boundary between Indian and Eskimo territory, whose summation of his life, as expressed to me, was: "It was an evil day for these people when I came among them."*

*The geography of the country is almost as interesting as the people and animals. This was the last retreat of the great, mile-thick glaciers* that relatively recently covered much of north-eastern America. Their titanic imprint remains as visible as if made only yesterday. Examples include the eskers running like monumental deserted railway embankments for hundreds of miles over a broken and shattered landscape of rocks and water; ancient marine beaches ringing hills at heights of several hundred feet and distances of several hundred miles from Hudson Bay – the last remnant of an enormous ocean that once covered the entire region.

These things are only scraps from the material I have to work with but may serve to illustrate the wealth of information I can draw upon.

Now down to cases. I appreciate your earlier suggestion that the first book should be primarily a personal narrative told in the first person, but I would like to keep myself out of it as much as possible. I want to let the Eskimos tell most of their own stories. I think this can be done with authenticity since one of my labours was the compilation of an Ihalmiut vocabulary, the doing of which made me at least somewhat familiar with their language. . . .

The book must have a heart and, equally vital, a purpose. The fate of the Ihalmiut is at the heart of the story, and the purpose is to draw attention to their plight and to that of all the native peoples of the north. And elsewhere, for that matter. So you can expect me to beat the drum about that quite a lot. But if it gets out of hand I am sure your editorial wisdom will find a solution.

I suspect this is a pretty poor sort of prospectus, but if it interests you enough to warrant even a tentative commission, it will have served. You understand, don't you, that I must write this book?

The time required to write it will depend on how well the Mowats manage to scrape a living during the book's gestation period but my guess is it will likely be as much as a year. An advance would be of great assistance of course but it will probably be necessary for me to hammer out a mess of pot-boilers too.

*You will suspect from the foregoing that I await your reply with great anticipation and no little trepidation. But please, Mr. Cloud, despite my sins of omission this past summer, don't keep me on tenterhooks too long.*

Farley Mowat

Urgently needing money, I now revised the short-story manuscript that had been rejected by *Atlantic Monthly* magazine and sent it away again – this time to *Maclean's* magazine in Toronto. I hoped it would do better in home waters. My anxiety about it mounted until a day in mid-November when Fran returned from a mail trip to Palgrave waving an envelope. It was a small envelope – too small to contain a rejected manuscript – and hope leapt within me as I tore it open. It contained a handwritten note from W.O. Mitchell, *Maclean's* fiction editor, inviting me to drop in to his office for a chat the next time I came to town. Nothing was said about my story.

Fran and I were on our way to Toronto a couple of hours later. I took a bath at the Thornhills' house, donned one of my father-in-law's clean shirts, and drove downtown to the formidable Maclean-Hunter building, having convinced myself that Nirvana was within.

W.O. Mitchell (his friends called him Bill) was a little older than I and had published a number of folksy short stories and radio plays, thereby becoming one of Canada's few successful writers. His recent appointment as fiction editor of *Maclean's* had been something of a coronation, yet he greeted the novice in friendly fashion, waved me to a comfortable chair, and suggested I light up as he searched for my manuscript amongst the papers cluttering his desk. Finding it, he sat back and, in the nicest possible way, blew me out of the water with a single salvo.

"Interesting little story you've got here. Unfortunately it doesn't really fit our needs. A little too grim. So I can't buy it but I *can* give you some useful advice."

He paused before delivering this.

"Fact is that what general circulation magazines like ours want these days is boy-meets-girl-three-thousand-words-with-a-happy-snappy-ending. You should bear that in mind."

With which he stood up and shook me warmly by the hand.

Torn between fury and despair, I drove to my father's office in the nearby provincial parliament buildings, where I subjected him to a blasphemous account of what had just happened to me. And he forever redeemed himself in my eyes by taking me to the nearby Mocamba Bar for a double rum and this apology.

"Sorry, old son, if I haven't seemed to be playing on your side these past months. I *was*, you know, but felt I had to keep it deep inside me.

"Truth is that what you were trying to do was what I had most wanted for myself after my war. And, well, I didn't have the ability, or maybe the guts, to carry it off. I was afraid you'd fail too. That's what I was trying to shield you from. But I was wrong to try. Dead wrong.

"It won't happen again."

Nor did it. From this time forward, Angus did almost everything he could to help me on my chosen way. (Almost, but that comes later.)

The first thing he did was to take me back to his office and give me a page torn from the American *Saturday Review of Literature*. It dealt with literary agencies in New York and especially sang the praises of one called Littauer and Wilkinson that specialized in finding markets for new writers breaking new ground.

"The hell with *Maclean's* – big frog in a little pond," my father said. "Send your Eskimo piece off to these people. What have you got to lose?"

It was a *very* long shot, but on the last day of November *Eskimo Spring* was in the mail again.

December of 1949 was as dour a month as any I have endured. The snows came early and fell heavily. Nevertheless, almost every day I made an attempt to get to the post office. There seldom was any mail, and nothing from New York – not even an acknowledgement of my submission. Nor was there anything from Boston – no ray of light anywhere.

We were now so hard up that I was debating with myself whether to ask my parents for a loan. As the snowdrifts mounted and our woodpile shrank, so did my hopes of making it at the writing game. I became seriously depressed – so much so that I even gave up the long walks on snowshoes Fran and I had been taking through the swamps and woods and over the wind-whipped hills.

Then, on December 21, Lulu Belle bucked her way through the drifts to Palgrave and the postmistress handed me an envelope bearing a U.S. stamp.

The letter it contained was short and sweet.

*Dear Mr. Mowat,*

*I'm glad to tell you that Saturday Evening Post has bought your excellent piece Eskimo Spring, which they will publish as The Desperate People. They are paying $500.00 of which our agency will take the usual 10%. The cheque will be in the mail this week.*

*We look forward to finding good homes for many more of your pieces.*

*Yours in serendipity,*
*Max Wilkinson*

# ˒ 3 ˒

# A BOOK IS BORN

We had a quiet Christmas. Snowfall was so heavy it immobilized even Lulu Belle, and, except on snowshoes, we were unable to go visiting or be visited. I was exhilarated by Max Wilkinson's coup, but distressed that for a long time I had heard nothing from Atlantic Monthly Press.

Although Dudley Cloud had initially written that the press was interested in a travel book from me "full of rich anecdotes and personal adventures," there had been no follow-up.

The year was coming to an end when I wrote him again.

*Mr. Dudley Cloud*                          *Dec. 29, 1949*
*Editor in Chief*
*Atlantic Monthly Press*
    *Dear Mr. Cloud:*
    *I have had no word from you about the outline for the arctic*

*book I sent you. I am a trifle concerned because I want to make a new expedition to the north for more material during the summer of 1950 but financial considerations will prevent me from doing so unless I can obtain some assurance of publication.*

*Mr. Wilkinson of the firm of Littauer and Wilkinson has kindly consented to act as my agent so if my book prospectus appeals to you would you be so very kind as to communicate with Mr. Wilkinson.*

*Best wishes,*

*Farley Mowat*

This time Cloud replied promptly and affirmatively but, rather than accepting my book and offering an advance against royalties (as was the norm), he proposed an option, for which he offered three hundred dollars.

I was delighted – yet disappointed. An option was no guarantee of commitment and, moreover, that much money would barely cover our ordinary living expenses for two or three months. It *was*, however, better than nothing so I accepted.

Cloud then sent me a succinct but definitive outline of what he expected the book to contain, including what amounted to a dissertation on method and purpose. Although smoothly phrased, his letter implied that the author's role was that of artisan, while the editor was effectively the architect.

My hackles rose. But I did not want to alienate the man who evidently considered himself in command of the project, and I contented myself with giving him some of my own thoughts about the proposed book.

*Dear Mr. Cloud:*                        *Jan. 16, 1950*

*So far I have written five chapters – and discarded four. Now I leave the typewriter alone for a few days while I cut firewood.*

*My information about the Eskimos is, as I have previously explained, by no means as complete as I would like. So I want to make another expedition to the Ihalmiut country but unless I obtain a good advance for the book I won't have funds to finance it. As my grandmother was fond of saying, "I am in a quarry about this."*

*I have come to the conclusion that I must divorce my personal "travel" experiences from the book. I have come to feel that the best way to write it is as a straightforward history of the people, explaining my presence in a foreword only. Since it is the Eskimos who are important to the story, and not myself, I think this is the best plan.*

*I think that the book should be as simple, as direct and unadorned as the life of the people it will try to portray. It will be no scientific treatise, nor will it be a "travel yarn" . . . it will begin with the genesis myth and then continue with the lives and history of the people from about 1850 until the present. My part in it will be that of narrator only. The central, tragic theme will therefore emerge in its own way without distortion.*

*Please let me have your reactions as soon as possible and in the meantime I will get back to work, even though the cellar leaks, our new dog is in heat, and my wife has stomach flu!*

*Cheerio,*

*Farley Mowat*

This letter crossed with one from Cloud in which, though he wrote with a velvet touch, he made it painfully clear who would set the rules. He dismissed *my* plan for the book in summary fashion.

Principles were at stake here but so was our livelihood. I bent to the wind and on January 21 returned the signed contract to Atlantic Monthly Press. I derived no joy from doing so. And received no applause. AMP took a month to acknowledge my surrender, and six weeks elapsed before I received the option fee.

It had been nibbled at. Ten per cent had been retained by

Wilkinson as the agent's fee, which was as it should have been. But fifteen per cent of the whole had been seized by the U.S. government as "alien income tax." After the exchange on the cheque had been paid, little more than two hundred remained.

On March 5 I wrote:

> *Dear Mr. Cloud:*
>
> *Yesterday I had a long letter from Mr. Wilkinson. It was in the nature of a lecture about the wisdom of heeding good advice. I went to bed and did some powerful thinking. The outcome is that I am scrapping my first six chapters and beginning again.*
>
> *Will send a progress report in a few weeks.*
>
> *Trust you are well.*
>
> > *Mowat*

I had, with great difficulty, masked my feeling, but nevertheless hoped my pique was showing. Then I began work on the book anew.

In July I bundled up what I had written (tentatively titled *River of Men*) and sent it to Dudley without a covering letter. The next move would be up to him.

That spring and summer I did a number of things to keep our pot boiling, including broadcasting six programs about the Ihalmiut on CBC Radio and writing six magazine pieces, five of which, together with another to *Saturday Evening Post*, Wilkinson sold. With or without a book, I was earning a living for us.

We also did a great deal of work about the house and property. It had always been my intention to become as nearly self-supporting as possible; now it was an imperative. That spring we planted a dozen fruit trees and prepared an enormous vegetable garden. In anticipation of a bumper crop, I dug and roofed a root cellar in which we eventually stored apples, cabbages, potatoes, turnips, carrots, onions, and squash. I also built a chicken house and run that we stocked with laying hens and pullets destined for the pot, and I made plans to excavate a pond in which to rear ducks and our own fish.

There were labours enough, but there were distractions too. On a whim I enrolled as a volunteer observer with the Dominion Meteorological Service, which supplied me with a sort of glorified doll's house on stilts containing maximum and minimum thermometers and apparatus for measuring rain and snowfall. This convenient "hive" attracted a swarm of bees and we might eventually have had our own supply of honey if the bees had not been so possessive that I had to evict them.

We also got to know our near neighbours better. Most of these were of the non-human variety, including salamanders, frogs, snakes, some of the more than a hundred species of birds we would eventually record, and over a dozen kinds of mammals ranging from Lilliputian water shrews to white-tailed deer who seemed to be of the opinion the vegetable garden was theirs. But visitors of the human kind also came by to distract and amuse us. Most were from afar, but some were local, dropping by occasionally to put us right on the finer points of country living. Initially I had had misgivings about attempting to make a life in rural Ontario but was now becoming more hopeful that it would work out. The mystery woman of the previous summer did not reappear, nor did Fran show any further interest in returning to Toronto.

That summer was blisteringly hot but with frequent rains so we got the bumper crop I had hoped for. The exhausted soil, fertilized with about fifty jeeploads of well-rotted manure from an abandoned farm, produced with such generosity that we filled the root cellar and could not even give away all the surplus.

The hens were laying well. My woodshed was bulging. The house was snug and welcoming. When, toward the end of October, I heard from Dudley Cloud again after a hiatus of nearly six months I found myself in no tearing hurry to reply.

*Dear Mr. Cloud:*              *Nov. 8, 1950*

*Thank you for your letter. I must admit to having felt some curiosity over the long silence that ensued when the new outline for "River of Men" went off into the blue.*

*It has been out of mind for some time now but I will keep your new list of suggestions before me and will endeavour to deal with them.*

*You ask about the theme. Put simply, it is an appeal for better understanding of the entire problem facing the survival of native people and an attempt to show it is impossible to bring such people into our world through a policy of cultural, physical, moral, and economic destruction. . . .*

*I too hope the "situation will develop" in a manner satisfactory to us all and in the not-too-distant future. My wife insists there is no need to exterminate her by slow starvation just to prove a point.*

*Best wishes.*

*Farley Mowat*

*Copy to Max Wilkinson.*

Cloud may have thought he had pushed me far enough, or perhaps he was reacting to a hint from Wilkinson that Atlantic had better offer me a contract or I might submit the manuscript to Dodd, Mead, another and larger American publisher, which was showing interest in it.

On December 10 Cloud wrote in friendly fashion, finally offering to publish *River of Men*, providing the offer was affirmed by his editorial board, which was dominated by the Boston publishing house of Little, Brown and Company, and assuming I was agreeable to some further "necessary" changes.

My reply was perhaps less enthusiastic than he may have anticipated.

*Dear Mr. Cloud:*                                       *Dec. 13, 1950*

*I am excited by the prospects for The River and only hope the Editorial Board agrees with you.*

*I am enclosing revisions for a new Foreword and Chapter 1. If this is not what you have in mind, perhaps you would enlighten me more specifically.*

*Have read much of the ms for the book once again (I enjoyed it!) but am not attempting any more revisions until I have seen your suggestions.*

*Best,*

*Farley Mowat*

Dudley evidently read me loud and clear. Only two or three days after hearing from me he wrote again, this time assuring me the editorial board's assent *would* be forthcoming and predicting that AMP/ Little, Brown *would* publish my book, assuming, of course, that we all agreed to some further "minor" revisions.

Although there was still no contract I concluded it was time to bite the bullet.

*Dear Dudley:*                                              *Jan. 10, 1951*

*I have by this mail sent off a new first chapter to Max, who will doubtless send it along to you pronto.*

*My wife, who has no shame in such matters, says she feels much good would come of a trip by the Mowats to Boston, at someone else's expense, of course. She means good for the Mowats.*

*You ask if I know W.O. Mitchell at* Maclean's *magazine. Answer is, not very well though I have tried to sell him stories. No luck. He turned 'em down and then Max sold them to SatEvePost. But a new editor at* Maclean's *did buy a short story from me.*

*I am also sending along a copy of my journal of my 1947 barrenland trip in case you think there might be a book in that.*

*F.*

To my enormous relief, a contract arrived for signing shortly after I had sent this letter. With it came a tentative invitation for Fran and me to visit Boston in March or April (a prospect that made Fran ecstatic), and an assurance the book would be published in the autumn of 1952.

Dudley also asked me to reply to a letter from a Mr. Mann – an American academic who had seen my first story in *Saturday Evening Post*.

Mr. Mann recommended that Atlantic have nothing to do with me. He accused me of concealing the fact that I had not been alone on my 1947 expedition and implied I was untrustworthy.

> *Dear Dudley:*                           *Jan 12, 1951*
>
> *Herewith the contract duly signed. Also my reply to Mr. Mann, who is a friend of Dr. Francis Harper, see below. I don't think I ever burdened you with the gen about my feud with Harper so here it is, in brief.*
>
> *In May of 1947 Harper, an American zoologist, and I went off together to Nueltin Lake to survey the fauna and the flora. He was under the auspices of the Arctic Institute, who paid his way. I was freelancing for the Royal Ontario Museum and paying my own shot.*
>
> *We had never met before and as it turned out we didn't get along any too well. It may be rude of me to say it but the old boy – he was my father's age – was minus some buttons. I was stupid enough not to realize it, and I took him seriously – for a while. But when he tried to convince me that slavery was the only solution to the "negro problem," and that it should be reaffirmed in the US South, I blew her! That's the trouble with being a rebel – you tend to lose your sense of humour just when you need it most. He wasn't quite so bad about Indians and Eskimos, but he just hated half-breeds or any sort of mixed bloods, and it turned out we had to spend a lot of time with a family of them at Nueltin Lake.*
>
> *The upshot was that he and I stopped talking. He'd sit on his side of the cabin and write me letters reflecting on the ancestry of the*

*Mowat clan (there are quite a bunch of Cree-Mowats in the Canadian north), which pissed me off more than a little. But I was at least smart enough not to pour fuel on the fire, and I took the first opportunity to go off travelling with one of the half-breeds. Which is how I got to spend time with the Ihalmiut.*

*To shorten a lamentable tale, he wrote to me after returning stateside telling me I was not to use his name in any way in any writing I might do. I was more than agreeable, and thought it was very nice of him to make it official. I trust you won't have many more Manns on your neck, but you may, in which case you can turn them over to me if you think it safe.*

*Glad you see something in my arctic journal. I feel a good travel book can come out of it – and not just a quickie follow-up to* River of Men *either.* * *Something distinctively different. Let me have it back as soon as possible so I can begin real work on it. And fear not that I will abandon all else once it is before me. I am already at work on a boys' book with two chapters rolled out.*

*On invitation from* Maclean's *new editor I'm doing a piece about my war that looks like potential material for a book. Strangely enough it would be a war book devoid of syphilitic soldiers and wholesale whoring. I sometimes feel the war I knew could not have been the same one many of my literary contemporaries apparently enjoyed. The men I soldiered with were pretty normal individuals who could actually think two consecutive thoughts that weren't concerned with women or booze. No doubt Jones, Vidal et al. would consider my lads quite abnormal – and perhaps they were. But I wonder if perhaps you publishers haven't conditioned the public to expect such juvenile excrescences from war writers? Something on this side of the Atlantic Ocean has certainly made it tough to portray men at war as Men, not large-gonaded adolescents.*

---

* No Man's River, *published in 2004 by Key Porter Books, Toronto, eventually came from this journal.*

*Fran is training me for our visit to Boston. Makes me wear shoes at least part of every day and I am no longer allowed to use the cutlery when searching for fleas. So do not fear, I shall not disgrace you and your good wife.*

*Cheers.*

*F.*

*Dear Dudley:*                                               *March 2, 1951*

*Have received your amended version of the MS and am dealing with suggested changes. I'm satisfied with most of the cutting and trimming you did, except I note you deleted all preliminary descriptive material about the Barrens so I have slyly reintroduced some of this. Perhaps I am wrong but it seems to me the reader might like to feel a little of the Rock of Ages between his finger tips before venturing into the land it came from.*

*Max has written to say he is expecting AMP's advance royalty payment and that my share – $540.00 – should soon be on its way.*

*Best wishes.*

*Farley*

The "amended version" of the manuscript had in fact been copy edited by Dudley's wife, Jeannette, and it was to her I wrote my next letter.

*Dear Mrs. Cloud:*                                          *March 19, 1951*

*Five days of solid labor (note spelling à la Webster) and the first six chapters are ready to be returned to you. But tell me, who is this fellow Webster who is now my Spelling Master? I've looked him up in my Encyclopaedia Britannica (1911 edition) and can't get a line on him.*

*I think it's a dirty trick anyway. For 29 years I've been labouring to spell correctly and am now told I have learned the wrong way. Dammit, Max says I punctuate like Chaucer, so why can't I be allowed to spell that way too?*

*Anyhow I've paid close attention to all the corrections you and Dudley have made, and have hunted out and slaughtered innumerable "thats."*

*Who is the Canadian publisher going to be? You know how anxious I am to have the book co-published in Canada by a Canadian company. No doubt this is all well in hand but I would appreciate being soothed.*

*F.*

March came and went, bringing no further news of a visit to Boston. In fact, I heard nothing more from Atlantic until late in April, when Dudley wrote, complimenting me for having put my book "into final shape for spring publication."

*Spring publication?* This was a bombshell. Hurriedly I read on and discovered to my chagrin and fury that my book, which had been slated for publication in the autumn of 1951 (in time for the Christmas trade) had, without anyone consulting me, been shifted to February of the succeeding year. *February* – the dead season in book publishing!

Dudley had tried to soften my reaction to this bad news by pointing out that Little, Brown might not be willing to publish my book at all if I insisted on being "obdurate" and demanding that the original publication date be adhered to.

The prospect of postponement was hard enough to bear. Worse followed in the next paragraph, where Dudley firmly scotched my hopes for co-publication with a Canadian company. Little, Brown, he wrote, "was adamantly opposed to relinquishing any portion of its exclusive North American rights." It intended to distribute the book in Canada under its own imprint, possibly but not necessarily through McClelland & Stewart. Furthermore, if I insisted on a Canadian imprint, Little, Brown could be expected to suspend publication "indefinitely."

Dudley refrained from telling me to shut up and back off but Max had no such compunctions. When he heard about this contretemps he wrote:

"If you insist on being difficult you had better find yourself another agent."

Something else was on his mind too. Both he and Dudley had been trying to interest me in writing an "action *novel*" about the north. "That," Max insisted, "would be as good as finding gold up there, could actually *be* about finding gold and could result in all of us finding a useful chunk of gold down here."

I now began to pull in my horns and wrote to Dudley.

> *Dear Dudley:*                          *May 12, 1951*
>
> *I guess your decisions about timing and about Canadian publication must prevail. Hell's bells, what do I know about the publishing business? And what could I do if I did?*
>
> *One thing I do agree with is that the name,* River of Men, *won't do. There have been too damn many Rivers published recently, but here is the best I can offer as an alternative.*
>
> *The Desperate People*
>
> *Inuit Ku (River of Men in Eskimo)*
>
> *People of the Deer*
>
> *Plains of Kaila*
>
> *Blood of the Barrens (Zane Grey would like that one).*
>
> *I have a number of small corrections to make on the setting copy for* What's Its Name. *However, there will no doubt be plenty of time to do that before Little, Brown publishes the book – if and when. . . .*

Communications between Dudley and me that summer were succinct and infrequent. In mid-summer I wrote:

*Working on a novel. Max holds what's left of the advance from River and doles it out parsimoniously. I'll bet you'd love to give me another advance on the next book? I'll bet!*

And again, in September:

*Dear Dudley:*

*It is to weep!*

*Corn borers, potato weevils, cabbage maggots, flea beetles, tomato worms, and grasshoppers are not enough for me to deal with? You want me to write some children's books, a novel, and – yuck – another book about the arctic too?*

*Yuck is what my Eskimo pal Ohoto always said when things got too much to bear.*

*Well, the novel is progressing – about 200 pages in rough draft – but still pretty nebulous.*

*It is set in Brochet – a small and very isolated northern community peopled by two Indian races, mixed-breeds of every degree, and a small group of whites including missionaries, free traders, H.B.C. traders, white trappers, and renegades.*

*The general theme is what happens to the taut balance between these groups when a small group of Canadian soldiers is dumped in by air in 1946 to establish a weather station and spy outpost.*

*Where does it go from here? God alone knows. When the first half dozen chapters are in better shape I'll send them along and you can draw your own conclusions.*

*I have considered your suggestion (or was it not mine?) of a boys' book. A book for young minds might do more to disseminate the truth about what has been going on in the north than can be dealt with by old and warty minds. So I will shortly send you an outline for a boys' book.*

*We took our annual holiday last week. Two days in Toronto. A movie, a Chinese dinner, and a ride on a streetcar. Fran, by the by, will be* *teaching at S.S. No. 12 this winter. It's a one-room schoolhouse on a lonely side road a couple of miles from us and will have something between five and eight students, mostly kids from the Catholic Children's Aid in Toronto who have been farmed out – literally – to impoverished local families. She'll get $40.00 a month, which will help keep us eating, if she can hack it. Wood stove for heat, but it does have an indoor john – a hole in the floor of the back hall, or rather 2 holes, one for boys and one for gals.*

We had had a good spring and summer and were slowly growing into the place and it into us. Repairing the damage done to the land by our predecessors was a priority. That spring Fran and I planted seven hundred young trees on our blighted hill – broad-leafed trees and conifers in what I thought was something like the original mix when this had still been primal forest.

I was determined to ensure lots of water so for a dollar I bought a battered, antique, horse-drawn drag bucket from a nearby farmer who had abandoned it in favour of a tractor. Then with Lulu's and Fran's help I began excavating a pond at the edge of the swamp. Fran drove the jeep, dragging the heavy iron scoop, which looked a bit like a giant sugar scoop except that instead of a single handle it was fitted with two stout wooden arms to which I clung while trying to steer the monster, and with which I could theoretically tip it up-and-over when it had dragged its load of muck out of the hole.

This was hot and heavy work. Lulu had a tendency to jolt forward, causing the wooden arms to sometimes heave me clean off my feet and catapult me over the bucket to land up to my ears in the slurry.

I also built a writing cabin that summer where I could sweat my brain instead of my muscles, and where I could mutter and curse without distressing Fran or the dogs, of which we now had three – Tegpa-the-Second and two of her male pups, Kipmik and Ohoto.

All the dogs showed remarkable tolerance for a vixen who was rearing a litter of cubs in a rock pile on our hill. No dog-fox was ever in evidence (I suspect he had been shot by one of the many hunters from Toronto who plagued the township). Kipmik would sometimes visit her den, very circumspectly, and we had seen him actually sniffing an especially forward fox cub, without the lurking vixen offering to interfere.

The garden tended to dominate our lives. The abundance and vigorous growth of our crop gave us the illusion we were wizards. It seemed we had but to throw seed of any kind in the ground, then stand back. I had doubled the size of the garden, which doubled the amount of work I had to put into it and trebled Fran's efforts to preserve a crop big enough to feed a dozen hungry mouths.

I particularly remember the Jerusalem artichokes. These tall, tough plants produce tubers that resemble dog droppings and probably have about the same nutritional value. The artichokes grew like wildfire and became a royal pain, not only because they were practically inedible but they were also virtually ineradicable. Even now – sixty years after I let them loose – they are still thriving even though all other vestiges of that garden have long since vanished.

Early in the autumn the gods of Modernity waved their wands and electricity came to us. As can be supposed, it revolutionized our way of life. Now we had running water – including running *hot* water; a bathtub that did not have to be filled and emptied with a bucket; and an indoor toilet that *flushed*. Or that *could* be flushed. However, since no sewer existed to which the toilet could be connected it remained out of action until I found the cash to buy a huge discarded oil tank to serve as a septic tank. I had it trucked to our place, dug an enormous hole in which to bury it and then a long trench to house the connecting pipe.

The evening I completed this task we celebrated by enjoying a ceremonial *indoor* flush.

But it rained all night – poured cats and dogs – and next morning when I looked out the window I beheld the septic tank in all its austere majesty *floating* on a pond of the rain's making. The tank had risen out of the earth like some spectral elevator because, as Lloyd happily pointed out, I had neglected to "pile a jeezly big pile of big rocks onto it to hold it down till it was pissed full."

Summer had been full of manual labours but I still managed to get a lot of writing done.

*Dear Dudley:*                                *Nov. 29, 1951*

*SatEvePost has bought a third yarn from me and* Maclean's *has bought a second one. The latter is about two guys wintering in a cabin away up north who got bushed and killed each other. No women, and hardly what you'd call a happy ending! Anyhow* Maclean's *has now commissioned a third piece, to be published next spring.*

*When I can't sleep at night I am reading* Fowler's Modern English Usage *on how to get rid of "thats." News that should cheer the hearts of you and your staff.*

*I recently got a telegram from* Atlantic Monthly Magazine *wanting photos of me for the cover of their January issue, in which they say there will be an excerpt from* People of the Deer.

*Me on the cover? Who do they think I am? Lana Turner? But please tell them: no more telegrams. You can't have the slightest idea what happens when a telegram hits Palgrave. Blacksmiths drop their horses! Millers, their mills. The village drunk is sober in the twinkling of an eye. Church bells peal out as if the Huns were coming. Then the whole bloody works come screaming over the Albion hills yelling: "Mr. Morfat! Mr. Morfat! . . . Come quick; somebody's dead!"*

*Yours in faith.*

*F.*

*Dear Dudley:*                                *Dec. 13, 1951*

*You ask about us being able to come south for a visit around pub-lication date. Well, Fran has quit the teaching trade so we are now available any time.*

*She has been muttering about Boston for two years so nothing short of the flux will stop her coming like a shot. To be honest I wouldn't take much persuading either.*

*Sorry if you have trouble reading this. My "liberated" Italian typewriter is on its last legs and I can't get ribbons that fit him. Guess I'll have to bite the bullet and buy a new typewriter though, as you doubtless realize, I can't really afford such a luxury.*

*Cheers for now.*

*F.*

Fran gave up teaching partly because her two Grade Eight students were fifteen-year-old male wards of the Catholic Children's Aid Society who became such ferocious competitors for her favours she was afraid they might kill one another, or her; and partly because she now thought (again mistakenly) that she was pregnant; it was illegal to teach in an Ontario public school while pregnant.

I *did* bite the bullet. I bought a new Underwood Standard for eighty dollars – a horrendous sum at that time. As happy as if it was a Rolls-Royce Phantom, I wrote to Dudley, revelling in the fact that what I typed was now generally legible.

*Dear Dudley:*                                               *Dec. 24, 1951*

*Much excitement at the prospect of a trip to Boston. Your kind offer to take us under your wing is greatly appreciated. As to costs – it all depends. If we travel by dog team they will be low, though I don't really know the cost of fish [dog feed] in the little towns en route. If we should decide to come by train I will ascertain the toll and let you know.*

*Sorry you are against the hero of my boys' book being a half-breed. I've polled a number of prospective younger readers and all like the idea. But then it is their parents who will buy the books, I suppose. My own parents have just adopted a five-year-old laddie named John whose mother is white and father is Indian but, and I say this without malice or smugness, we seem to have less feeling about "colour" up here.*

Maclean's *wants an article about some rather fantastic experiences I had toward and after the end of the war in Europe. In looking over the material, I was forcibly reminded that it had always been my intention to do a war book, if only as an antidote to the adolescent literary bullshit which has come to be accepted in North America as the soldier's view of World War II.*

The early months of 1952 would see the publication in *Atlantic Monthly* of three excerpts from *People of the Deer*. A foretaste of the jubilation that would be mine came on January 24 when I received an advance copy of the book itself. I wrote exultantly to my editor.

> *Dear Dudley:*
>
> *A virginal POD was waiting at the post office yesterday. By 8:00 P.M. Fran and I had staked a claim on the Park Plaza bar in Toronto and the wolves were howling!*
>
> *Excelsior! And Eureka! It is, in truth, one hell of a fine job of bookmaking you've all done and by God I'm proud as hell to be F. Mowat. There'll never be another moment like this one. Thank you, friends.*
>
> *By way of a small return I can report progress with the second draft of the boys' book. Four new chapters done, so the plug is out and I hope to bring you a complete MS when we come down.*
>
> *The editor-in-chief of Michael Joseph in London has written a glowing letter confirming that they are going to publish POD in England. I am well into its follow-up, a version of my Barrenlands journal book that should give the reader a better idea of the non-human elements of the Barrens – the birds and the bees as it were. I have no desire to become an arctic specialist, but first I have to get that country out of my literary system.*

*I'm banging away at a wolf chapter for it and we'll see if Max can sell that as a magazine piece. You asked about the new book's "specific purpose." Well, I guess it's an attempt to reconnect mankind (i.e., the poor bloody reader) with Mama Nature. . . . I'd like it to reveal a little truth about the usually misunderstood, much-maligned, yet tremendously attractive relatives of ours ranging from lemmings to loons and everything in between. Comprenez-vous? Maybe I'm being Schweitzerish. Sanctity of Life and all that. Why not? I've seen enough of the other side, God knows.*

*I'll work on this till March 2 which is D-Day for us. Departure Day. The Saturday night train from Toronto gets us to Boston Sunday at 9:00 A.M. Fare is $56 per bod return, not counting berths. Does this suit?*

*Could you let me know the sched for the promotional trip to New York? If your people could find us a small room in an inexpensive little hotel then we might stay on in N.Y. a few days after the Little Brown men (are they really little brown folk?) of the advertising department are through with us. At our own expense, of course.*

The official publication date for *People of the Deer* was February 26, but review copies had been sent out a month earlier, and the first review appeared on February 24 in the *New York Times Review of Books*. Written by a schoolteacher who, in the 1930s, had spent part of a summer canoeing north of Reindeer Lake, it was dismissive of my venture.

This review was followed by an outright attack on me in *The Beaver*, the house organ of the Hudson's Bay Company, in which I was accused of being a know-nothing, if not an outright liar.

Max hastened to warn me that these first reactions had ruffled a lot of feathers at Atlantic Monthly Press and Little, Brown and Company.

*Atlantic is getting irate letters from so-called northern experts claiming you are full of it. Maybe that should be past tense because a hell of a lot of "it" seems to have already hit the fan.*

*You may have to hunker down in a slit trench for a while. But have no fear. Not only is the Lord righteous, He is also a bibliophile and will doubtless come to your rescue. Meantime the publicity gener-ated by these lummoxes will rebound upon them by selling lots of books for us.*

As I wrote to Dudley, the roof seemed to be falling in.

*Your three telegrams and letter arrived yesterday. Not quite a bolt from the blue, but like enough. The balloon is going up and it is a mite scary. Seems I have taken on some rather imposing adversaries: the Roman Catholic and Anglican Churches, the Government of Canada, and at least one very large and wealthy business corporation.*

*Wonder if I'll get crucified. Or just boiled in oil. I'm even wonder-ing if my proposed boys' book might bring the World Institute for Child Welfare down on my neck too.*

*The raking over the coals in the* New York Times *is actually pretty trivial. Its author makes me out to be untrustworthy mainly because he claims I have mistranslated some Chipewyan place names and have neglected to list every previous white man to have found his way into the Barrenlands, including himself although he never got closer than its southern edge.*

*I've pounded out a reply which I'll get off to the editor of the* Times Review *in a couple of days. Maybe they'll publish it – maybe not. It ends like this:*

*Mr. Downes evidently feels I should have written a scholarly compendium of facts about this obscure part of the world. Let me put him straight. I am no pedant and make no claim to being a scholar. Abstract facts, real or contrived, selected to serve a purpose, do not concern me half as much as do the stories of living people and the difficulties they encounter in trying to survive.*

*This is what my book is all about.*

*I've also enclosed a reply to* The Beaver *piece. This is a different matter. I've taken the H.B.C. to task in no uncertain manner so they have every reason to counterattack. Don't know how it will end. An individual has never successfully taken on the H.B.C. (Here Before Christ, it's called in the arctic), though many have tried. This* Beaver *piece is a warning shot across our bows. When they've seen the whole book they'll bring up the big guns, so stand by for action!*

*See you Sunday, and it won't be in church.*

*F.*

On March 2 Fran and I caught the night train from Toronto. Jeannette and Dudley welcomed us at the Boston station. Dudley was an expansive, pipe-smoking Labrador, while Jeannette was an effusive and well-coiffed chow. Instead of parking us in a hotel, they gave us the run of their own warren in an ancient building on venerable Pickney Street and treated us as rare birds from another world.

Next day at a cocktail party in our honour, we were exhibited to the staffs of Atlantic Monthly and Atlantic Press, whose curiosity about us seemed as great as if we had come from Patagonia. Most knew little about Canada but were very curious about the "North," which word they pronounced as if with a capital N.

Anxious to oblige, I told stories about Eskimo life and entertained with demonstrations of Eskimo string figures. Some of these were very explicit, especially one called (my translation): Horny-dog-screwing-snotty-bitch-whose-feet-are-froze-to-the-ice.

We were also put on display at a glittering dinner party given by Arthur Thornhill, president of Little, Brown and Company, for

Boston's publishing elite. Arthur was of the bull mastiff type, with bloodshot eyes and bad halitosis. He did not endear himself to me with his introductory speech, which began:

"We at Little, Brown believe writers are of considerable importance . . ."

To make up for this, Dudley, who was a dedicated woodworker, took me to his favourite tool shop where I blew most of our budget on Swedish-steel handsaws and English-made wood chisels.

Jeannette took Fran to Fileen's Bargain Basement in downtown Boston, where my wife was mesmerized by a plethora of marked-down goodies culled from the giant department store's vast selection but had not the wherewithal to do much about it.

After three days of being fêted in Boston, we were put on another train and sent to New York, where we were astonished and somewhat intimidated to find ourselves booked into the Algonquin Hotel, the venerable establishment that was the favourite watering place for such luminaries as the *New Yorker's* Dorothy Parker and James Thurber and for visiting literary giants from overseas. We were suitably impressed, although most of our stay was spent shuttling between bookstores and radio stations (television was then still in diapers even in New York), enduring an early version of what would become the ritual book promotion tour of later years.

We enjoyed one memorable evening with Max Wilkinson, an ebullient if somewhat lecherous lamb in wolf's clothing. On our final evening we were guests of honour at a dinner party held in the Algonquin's renowned Oak Room. In attendance were several free-loading literary critics who, as I noted in my journal:

> . . . *gave me a royal pain, patronizing Fran and me to a fare-thee-well while making it clear Canada and Canadians were of less concern to the Master Race than Hottentots were to the British Raj. One fat-assed bastard actually proposed this toast: "Someday your little*

*country may get to join the States – something it should have done a couple hundred years ago."*

By the time Fran and I got home to Albion, the frost was coming out of the ground and the 30th side road was again impassable. Nevertheless, this was a wonderful spring. The skies were high and bright, and the returning sun warmed everybody's blood, including that of our resident fox snake who, having hibernated in the foundation of our fireplace chimney, now came out the wrong hole to find himself in our living room. There he cowed our dogs and gave Fran a bad few moments, buzzing his tail and baring non-existent fangs as he pretended to be a rattlesnake.

Next day we were privy to a show put on by a pair of porcupines smitten by spring fever. I found them in a spruce tree in our swamp, nose to nose on a horizontal branch quite literally screaming at each other with such intensity they could be heard half a mile away. But it was love not rage they were expressing. When they had sung themselves out they settled down to business – in the missionary position, but standing up.

Incidents like these, together with the return of migrant birds ranging from hummingbirds to turkey vultures; the chirruping and galumphing of toads and frogs in the swamp and ponds; and, in general, the all-pervasive aura of hell-for-leather sex permeating woods and waters; plus the relentless demands of gardening and of planting another thousand treelets, left me little time for my profession.

I did not get in touch with Dudley again until spring was almost over.

*Dear Dudley:*　　　　　　　　　　　　　　　　　*May 29, 1952*
*I've been too busy to write these last several weeks because the debtor's prison has been hanging over my head, but now all is rosy again. Max has sold another story for me and the garden is up.*

*My peas are six inches high, my onions are edible, and radishes too, despite being nibbled by flea beetles. The woods and swamps are producing a bounty of wild leeks, fiddlehead ferns, and morel mushrooms. Our hens are laying like bloody mad. Soon we shall be independent of the cruel world of commerce.*

*Surprisingly the Governor General's Literary Award Commission (Christ, what a mouthful) has picked me to get a medal for the best short story by a Canadian in 1951. It's the one W.O. Mitchell and Maclean's turned down!*

*Jack McClelland of McClelland and Stewart has finally awakened to the fact they are supposed to be my Canadian publishers and everything is hunky-dory between us. He and I call each other pet names and drink out of the same glass. Also, Max tells me that POD is the non-fiction choice of the Book Society in Britain, so all seems lovely in my literary garden.*

*The multiplicity of things to be done this spring have kept me away from the Machine, but a draft of the wolf story is with Max, who now says he likes it very much. The first time he saw it, back in 1950, it made him gag. But since then I have learned that flippancy and coyness are not my forte.*

*The boys' book nears completion and I've sold another yarn to SatEvePost so we can afford to eat store food again. I'm beginning to think Canadian writers who have to live by their trade can only succeed in doing so by selling their wares to magazines. Publishing books has to be just a sideline. I also note that I am one of the very few independent writers in this country who makes his full-time living by writing. Sort of.*

Another letter followed in early June.

*We go to London (our London, on our Thames here in Ontario) on Friday to collect my lead medallion. No cash, of course. This is*

*Canada! The bastards expect me to show up in full dress and, by God, don't even offer to pay the travel expenses involved. I shall wear worn-out mukluks and a worm-eaten caribou parka and if that gives His Excellency peptic ulcers they'll have nobody to blame but themselves.*

The investiture was staged in the ballroom of the Hotel London. Trumpeted as the most significant literary event ever held in Canada, it was presided over by Governor General Vincent Massey, one of the country's wealthiest men, and it gave Canada's "best" writers a free dinner and a medal but nothing else.

Not even free drinks.

*Earle Birney, winner of the poetry award; sports writer Scott Young; and some other "literary scribes," as we were later stigmatized, adjourned to the men's washroom of the hotel, where we played a kind of bowling game by rolling our medals into the urinals (each of which we had numbered) ranged against the far wall of the lavatory. The prize for the highest score was to have been a bottle of rum donated by Blair Fraser, one of Maclean's editors; but we ended by sharing it in a series of decidedly irreverent toasts to the organizers of the affair.*

On June 27 the mail contained a clipping from the summer issue of *The Beaver*, sent to me by a friend who had scrawled across it:

*In case you ain't seen this yet. Keep your head down, chum!*

"This" was a bombshell disguised as a review, written by an employee of the federal government and published in the Hudson's Bay Company's *Beaver*, intended to blow both me and *People of the Deer* into the dustbin. The author was A.E. Porsild, a botanist with the Canadian Museum of Nature and on this occasion spokesman for the federal Department of Northern Affairs. At three thousand words, the piece was quite the longest "review" ever published by *The Beaver*, but no space was wasted on literary matters.

Porsild devoted himself to discrediting what I had written about the fate of the Ihalmiut and other inland-dwelling Inuit while accusing me of inventing scurrilous nonsense about legitimate businesses such as the Honourable Company of Merchant Adventurers (the Hudson's Bay Company's official title). Moreover, according to him I had maliciously maligned the several arms of government charged with caring for native peoples, together with the selfless Roman Catholic and Anglican missionaries who had dedicated their lives to bringing Light into Darkness in the North.

Porsild went on to suggest I had spent only a few weeks in the Barren Lands and that, if the Ihalmiut ever *had* existed outside my imagination, they could never have been numerous enough to warrant such a hue and cry as I had raised. He assured his readers there was no truth in my book – and precious little in me either. The "review" concluded by bestowing upon me a pseudo-Inuit title: *Sagdlutorssuaq* – Teller of Tall Tales.

I soon discovered that copies of this issue of *The Beaver* had been sent to all the prominent newspapers and magazines in Canada and the United States, together with a covering letter implying that I had perpetrated a hoax on the public. One of these incendiary bombs was received by Ontario's Minister of Education, accompanied by a request that *People of the Deer* be removed from Ontario school libraries on the grounds that it was "a work of fiction."

I had been anticipating trouble, but not on this scale. I wrote to Dudley.

> *It's taken a few days to stop the tremor in my limbs – not of fear, but of rage! This is a major counterattack which is bound to have considerable adverse effect. I've written a rebuttal, but* The Beaver *is only published quarterly so even if they print my reply, which they*

*probably won't, it will be too late even to limit the damage. The Montreal Star has already done an editorial echoing Porsild and I expect the rest of the establishment will follow that line.*

*Hugh Kane at McClelland and Stewart tells me the H.B.C. is spreading the story they are going to sue me and the publishers but he says they won't really do it – just bluffing to make us keep quiet. Hope he's right.*

Ten days later I wrote again:

*Hugh Kane has been in touch with the H.B.C. They say they don't intend to print my reply. When Kane asked them to print a paid ad for the book in which the more salient points of my reply would appear they refused to do that either.*

*It's been suggested I start a libel suit against them but this seems impossible for financial reasons and because the Bay would appeal again and again until I was too broke to stand upright.*

*Perhaps I am taking this all too seriously, but it is certainly not doing my disposition any good. Frankly, I am getting so upset about the whole affair that my writing is grinding to a halt. So where do I go from here?*

Dudley's advice was that I get back to work and bury myself in a new book until the storm blew over. I partly did as he suggested, but the work I chose had nothing to do with writing. I decided to leave that strictly alone until sufficient scar tissue had formed. Instead I built a workshop-cum-garage where I could fool around making furniture or doing maintenance on Lulu Belle. I also enlarged our house, which had been cramped to start with and would be even more so when we started a family. I added a wing containing one large and one small bedroom.

By the end of August, I had almost succeeded in pushing the

*People of the Deer* imbroglio to the back of my mind. However, in September it came thundering out again when fellow freelance writer Scott Young sent an op–ed piece called "Storm out of the Arctic" to the Toronto magazine *Saturday Night*.

Young's piece was not so much concerned with buttressing my accusations against the northern establishment as with my right, indeed obligation, to make such charges. However, without inform-ing Young, *Saturday Night's* editor, R.A. Farquharson, sent a copy of "Storm" to Dr. Porsild, at the same time offering him three pages of the magazine in which to reply. Both pieces appeared, side by side. Scott was outraged, especially so when Farquharson denied him space for a subsequent rebuttal.

While Scott fumed, I dashed off a response of my own. It read, in part:

> *No anthropologist in Canada or elsewhere has attacked my book. Botanist Dr. Porsild is the sole academic or scientific accuser. A formida-ble list of reputable authorities, including Dr. Ralph Linton, chairman of Yale University's Department of Anthropology; Dr. Wm. S. Carlson, president of the University of Vermont and leader of the Fourth Greenland Expedition; Vilhjalmur Stefansson, renowned arctic explorer; Lord John Tweedsmuir, one-time arctic trader for the Hudson's Bay Company; Dr. E. Carpenter, an expert on Eskimo ethnology at the University of Toronto; and Mr. Hugh MacLennan, one of Canada's fore-most writers, have given their support to my book and to my contentions in whole or part, and the majority of them have done so in print.*
>
> *Furthermore, in 1951 the "non-existent" Ihalmiut were visited by M.J. Michea, an anthropologist from the French National Museum who is now preparing a monograph on the Ihalmiut. M. Michea has been kind enough to give me a statement that in his opinion my book is accurate in all important aspects, and that it is the best study of an Eskimo group he has ever read.*

*It has proved impossible to obtain information about the current state of the Ihalmiut from official sources which continue to claim that the Ihalmiut do not exist. However, contacts in the Canadian military, which has established a weather station at Ennadai Lake in the centre of the Ihalmiut country, report that, as of mid-1952, twenty-seven Ihalmiut still survived but that their condition was deplorable and they were existing principally on handouts from the soldiers, who appear to be showing a good deal more humanity than has our government.*

*Perhaps after all the Ihalmiut are no more than ghostly shadows who can be erased from existence, and from history, in order that men of little conscience can sleep easier.*

Mr. Farquharson's reaction to this, and to a second letter from me, was this refusal to print either of them:

*Obviously if we run your letters we are duty bound to show them to Porsild first, so you can understand why we do not wish to continue this controversy.*

To my surprise (and undeniable relief) the public paid little attention to this new assault upon *People of the Deer* and its author. In fact, by the end of November the entire ruckus seemed to have receded as harmlessly as summer lightning.

There was, however, a brief eruption in the House of Commons in mid-January 1953, when the Member of Parliament for Saskatoon, Robert Knight, queried the Honourable Jean Lesage, Minister of Resources and Northern Affairs, about my book. The following direct quotation is from *Hansard*.[*]

---

[*] *The official verbatim record of the House of Commons, vol. 96, no. 31, Tues. Jan. 19, p. 1243, etc.*

Mr. Knight: . . . *The last time this subject was under discussion I brought to* [the Minister's] *attention certain allegations that had been made in "People of the Deer" by Farley Mowat. I think that at that time the Minister said he would look into the subject . . . if the allegations in the book are true it is a terrible indictment of neglect upon the part of somebody.*

[Mowat's] *allegations were that a certain tribe of Eskimos have been allowed, through various circumstances, to disintegrate and that in fact their numbers were decreased and depleted through starvation. . . . I should like to know if the Minister has anything to tell us about it. It is a rather serious business. It involves the lives of people. It involves their extermination by starvation. . . . What are the comments of the Minister upon the whole situation . . . ?*

Mr. Lesage: *I said, and I do not believe I can say anything more,* [the book] *is false, the allegations are false. If the Hon. Member wishes to have a detailed criticism* [Porsild's review] *of that book indicating the extent to which the information upon which the book is based is false, I am sure that my office and my Deputy Minister* [the man who had fired me from the government service when Fran and I were at Brochet] *would be delighted to send it to the Hon. Member. . . . There is nothing more false than that part of the book which says that a certain tribe was allowed to perish by starvation. There is no grounds at all for that allegation. . . . I do not have in mind all the facts concerning the allegations in this book but I shall be delighted to have an officer give the Hon. Member all the information he requires in order that his soul, as a Member of Parliament, may be at peace, and that he will not believe he has been at fault in allowing starvation to occur in this country without any measures being taken against it.*

Mr. Knight: *Since the Minister has said categorically that these things are false, I should like to say that I too have*

*information from what I consider to be a fairly competent author-
ity stating that such allegations are largely true. . . .*

Mr. Lesage: *At the time the book was written and the events
occurred to which my Hon. Friend has referred, I was not very
well versed in either northern affairs or Eskimo affairs. However
I am now informed by responsible officers in my Department that
the information in the book is false. . . . My officers are in a position to satisfy* [Mr. Knight] *that there was no delay by the proper
officers in doing what was necessary to cope with an emergency.*

Mr. Knight: *I think it would be wise if the information which
the Minister asserts his officers can give were to be given publicly
to the whole country.*

Mr. Adamson [a government M.P.]: *Would it be possible to
have Dr. Porsild's monograph on the subject given to those
members who may be interested in it?*

Mr. Lesage: *I thank the Hon. Member for his suggestion . . .
and I will see to it that Dr. Porsild's monograph is mimeographed
and distributed to them. This would be one of the best answers to
the allegations in the book "People of the Deer."*

Mr. Knight: *Let me suggest that in all fairness if Dr. Porsild's
statement is to be made public then the reply by Mr. Mowat
should be made public so that the Hon. Members can come
to their own conclusions. . . . If the government is going to mimeograph Dr. Porsild's reply at public expense, then I suggest
that it should mimeograph the other at the same time. Does
not the Minister consider that this would be the fair way to
handle the matter?*

Mr. Lesage: *I do not want to enter into this controversy and
I can see no reason at all why we should perpetuate it. And under
the circumstances, since the Hon. Member objects, nothing will
be mimeographed.*

———

Although attempts to discredit *People of the Deer* wound down thereafter, Dr. Porsild fired a belated final shot that he presumably believed would prove mortal. Upon discovering the book had received the Anisfield-Wolfe Award for "its contribution to improved understanding of aboriginal problems," Porsild, in his capacity as a Canadian government official, wrote to the chairman of the Anisfield-Wolfe Foundation in the United States.

> *I am sure Farley Mowat is pleased with the award and perhaps a little amused too that his "plea for the understanding help without which these people will vanish from the earth" has been heard.*
>
> *What worries me is that the Ihalmiut people never did exist except in Mowat's imagination.*

During the next several years, I spent much time investigating the final fate of the Ihalmiut and the rest of the inland Inuit who, at the beginning of the century, had numbered as many as two thousand individuals and had inhabited a quarter of a million square miles of northern Canada.

Encouraged and even harassed by Jack McClelland, in 1959 I published my findings in *The Desperate People*, a book that provides the grim details of what I believe to have been an act (even if an inadvertent one) of genocide.

My opponents and detractors took a different tack with this new book. As Jack explained to a meeting of his sales staff that I attended:

"They're keeping their heads down this time, and their mouths mostly shut. They've figured that if there's no fur flying the press won't pick up the story and it'll die. Public interest will evaporate like spit on a hot plate. And the smartasses in Ottawa and in the missions and big business have got it right this time."

Grinning lopsidedly at me through a haze of tobacco smoke, he summed it up.

"I hate to say this, Farley, but this book's going to get the treatment those poor sods *in* it got: burial in an unmarked grave!"

Jack's prediction proved accurate and the desperate people's unmarked graves might well have disappeared forever had it not been for an incident that occurred four decades later.

In 1987, press lord Conrad Black added the venerable Toronto literary magazine *Saturday Night* to his stable. Black chose Kenneth Whyte to be *Saturday Night's* new editor, and Whyte immediately set about trying to turn the elderly magazine into a money-making tabloid of the attack-dog variety. After printing a venomous "exposure" of a teenager who was devoting himself to a worldwide movement dedicated to helping disadvantaged youngsters, the "new" *Saturday Night* moved on to bestow a Judas kiss upon the political aspirations of a woman member of the federal parliament.

Then they had a go at me.

Early in 1996, Anna Porter, publisher of Key Porter Books, was asked to cooperate in preparing a feature "profile" of me for a forthcoming issue of *Saturday Night*. Since Key Porter was my publisher at the time and about to publish a new book of mine, Anna was happy to oblige and assumed I would be too.

Although my earlier experience with this magazine had not led me to regard it with much affection, I made myself available to be interviewed by the man hired to write the piece. My wife and I invited him to our home (where he shared our hospitality without giving any intimation that he carried a knife under his shirt). I also arranged for him to have extensive access to the Farley Mowat archives at McMaster University.

Stupidly, I did not realize anything was amiss until *Saturday Night* wanted a portrait taken of me. This resulted in a most peculiar photographic session in an abandoned Toronto warehouse where I was costumed, posed, and lighted as if for a portrait of Dracula. Even then (although I now had an uneasy feeling about the whole affair)

I did not realize I had been set up until the May issue of the magazine appeared, with me on its cover wearing a sinister expression and an enormous Pinocchio nose.

There was worse inside.

The "profile" turned out to be a character assassination constructed largely from the canards the Hudson's Bay Company, Porsild and various government officials, and others had spread about me during the imbroglio over *People of the Deer*. The intent of the piece was now crystal clear – it was meant to bury *me*.

Some of my partisans thought I should sue, but others who had crossed swords with Conrad Black's empire (and who had the scars to prove it) persuaded me that suing him or his minions would be a feckless enterprise unless I possessed his seemingly bottomless pockets.

In the end, it hardly mattered. Whyte's venture into yellow journalism proved of small benefit to the magazine. Quite the opposite. Within a few years, *Saturday Night* itself was dead and buried . . . some called it suicide.

# , 4 ,

## SPREADING MY WINGS

One splendid day in 1952, I was in the garden digging potatoes and trying to rid my mind of the turmoil induced by the *People of the Deer* affair, when a car drove up our long laneway and out of it clambered a man I had last seen eight years before on a battlefield in Italy.

The Rev. Frederick Goforth, wartime chaplain with the Hastings and Prince Edward Regiment, had sought me out with a job proposal.

"I've not come to yarn about old times, Squib [my army nickname], though I don't doubt we'll get around to that. Fact is, you've made such a bang with your Eskimo book that the Regimental Association, of which I'm chairman, would like you to have a go at writing the story of the Hasty Ps. Stories, I guess, because nearly four thousand good men served with us during the late, unholy bloodbath.

"Most, like you and me, made it home, though as you well know a good many came back shot full of holes. And a good many more joined the White Battalion over there and are never coming back.

"We'd like you to tell their story so, just maybe, *they* won't be forgotten with the rest, as the poem says."

Freddy Goforth had caught me off guard but I was not unreceptive. For a long time I had been considering a book based on my wartime experiences and had even written Dudley Cloud and Max Wilkinson to see how they felt about it.

They had not been favourably inclined then, but after Freddy's visit I wrote them again.

> *My old army outfit wants me to write its history in World War II and say they'll pony up $3,000.00 expense money if I'll have a go. It might provide a God-given opportunity for me to soak up material and atmosphere that would be invaluable for the war novel I've had in mind. What say you now?*

Max replied with a kindly but adamantine rejection.

> *I don't doubt you'd write a powerful book but the market down here is sinking under a flood of war books and one more, especially by a Canuck, would go down like a lead balloon. Forget it, laddie!*

Dudley took his time replying but, when he did, was equally negative.

> *There may be a market for such a book in Canada. There would be none in this country where most folk probably don't even know Canadians were in the war unless it was as cannon fodder for the British. I beseech you to put this idea out of mind and continue writing about the North, which usually gets a good response from American readers.*

Discouraged but not convinced, I approached several Canadian publishers. Only one showed interest – Jack McClelland, who responded quickly:

> *If the people in Boston don't want a war book from you let us look at it. And let us get together and discuss the matter in a civilized manner as soon as possible. I suggest the rooftop bar of the Park Plaza, where the rum is nearly as good as the Pusser kind we used to gargle in the navy.*

Soon thereafter, I was able to phone Freddy Goforth and tell him McClelland & Stewart seemed game to publish the book if I would write it.

As our third winter in Albion began, blizzards and snow-blocked roads provided an illusion that I was out of the line of fire in the skirmishes that were still erupting around *People of the Deer*. Nevertheless, I could not concentrate on a new writing project, probably because I was suffering from a kind of literary shellshock that made it difficult for me to write anything that might involve me in new hostilities. I was, however, able to relieve my writer's itch by turning to my personal journal.

Keeping journals is much less demanding than writing for publication. There is no need to equivocate or be evasive, and the results do not need to be primped, powdered, or rouged so as to pass muster with editors or literary critics. In January of 1953 my journal was my literary life raft.

> *Jan. 14  Feeling lousy. Can't concentrate worth a god damn. Have started about a dozen short pieces and three books since last autumn and they've all died still-born. I'm chock full of words but all I can produce is unsatisfactory farts. I can't even write about the birds and the bees without sneaking a look over my shoulder to see if some irate*

*hunter might be figuratively drawing a bead on me, which is a damned shame because if it wasn't for the example of the non-human creatures I suspect I might become as virulently bellicose and bloodthirsty as all too fucking many of my fellow men. Bad cess to the lot of them!*

*Jan. 20  As if I wasn't already in deep shit, I'm surrounded by even deeper piles of it. Not my own this time though. Almost every farm around here has one or two lads from the Toronto Catholic Aid living on it. Families get paid a few bucks a month to keep these kids, orphans from ten years old on up, a lot of whom get their asses worked off and otherwise aren't much better treated than house slaves from Uncle Tom's Cabin country a hundred years ago. But what really makes me want to oil up my gun is that they get used as bum-boys by anyone takes a fancy to them.*

*There's one of the bung-holers only half a mile from us. Teaches at Upper Canada College and has bought himself a rundown farm out here as a get-away place where he can sculpt "the glories of the human form," is what he says. He pays his subjects nickels and dimes and bribes their keepers with booze and cash to let him draw these kids, stark staring naked. And do other things. The kids don't bitch because if they did they'd end up back at the Aid in Toronto, where life could get even worse. Or so they tell me.*

*The hell of it is there doesn't seem to be a damn thing Fran and I can do about it. Other than let the bum-fucker know we're on to him. The cops don't want to hear about it. Neither does anybody else I've talked to. It's a See-no-evil situation with a capital S. We have befriended some of the lads, including a few who are savvy enough to steer clear of the bugger, like Murray Biloki, a good-looking kid who knows what's what and maybe will amount to something some day but many of the Aid's kids haven't a snowball's chance in hell of keeping clear.*

*Damned if I can understand how we self-appointed Lords of the Universe can be so fucking rotten to those of our own kind who are just barely able to stay afloat because they've been kicked about like horse turds. And why don't the rest of us holier-than-thou hypocrites have the guts to do what needs to be done about it?*

*C'est la guerre, eh? No, by Jesus, c'est la humanité.*

Although March roared in with icy gales and blustery snowstorms, my spirits began to lift when the mail brought a formal contract from the Regimental Association. And then, soon afterwards, an envelope containing a cheque for three thousand dollars – by far the largest sum of money I had ever possessed.

A few days after depositing this cheque, Lulu Belle and I drove off on the first of what would be many visits to the counties of Hasting and Prince Edward, journeys that would introduce me to the pre-war world of the men I had fought beside and whose lives and deaths would be the substance of my next book.

Also that March, businessmen in the nearby town of Bolton formed a company to bring the telephone to Albion Township. Wires were strung, and soon one of the magic machines encased in its varnished wooden box was mounted on our kitchen wall. It was brought to life by lifting the receiver attached to one side of the box then rotating a hand crank on the other side, thereby sending a signal to the operator in Bolton. When and *if* she responded, you gave her the name of the exchange and the number of the party you wanted to reach and, quite often, you got through.

This being a party line shared by fourteen families, incoming calls were identified by a ring code. Ours was two long and three short rings from two large bells which crowned the box. Their shattering tones could be heard a hundred yards away. Especially in the early days, this strident summons proved virtually irresistible to every family on our line, regardless of whose number was being rung. One by one, all or most of the receivers would be snatched from their hooks but, as each was lifted, the voltage on the line would drop until the voice of the caller would be reduced to an eerie whisper.

As if this was not trouble enough, few of the listeners-in could resist the temptation to interject their own comments and observations into what were supposed to be private conversations. Pleas for privacy were generally ignored – until I hit upon a way to clear the line.

Andy Lawrie, who had worked with me in the north, called up one day. Our conversation soon began to lose the battle with the voltage drop and the associated heavy breathing from the listeners-in, not all of whom restricted themselves to passive interference.

"*Speak up*, can't you!" demanded a testy voice I identified as belonging to widow Jane Finnerty. Then, "Charlie, you old fool, turn down your radio! I can't hardly hear what that Mowat fellow's saying!"

It was then that inspiration struck. Remembering that Andy specialized in parasitology, I launched into a shouted description of a human parasite I had recently been reading about.

"Called the guinea worm," I bellowed into the mouthpiece. "Only as big around as a pencil lead but grows up to ten feet long. Burrows all through your body and every now and again crosses one of your eyeballs. That's the one time you can do anything about it.

"The natives have figured *what* to do. They take a stick and split one end, then slide the worm's body into the cleft. Then – and here's the tricky bit – you gradually wind the worm onto the stick. The victim has to do this himself, or herself, because it has to be done slow as molasses. It can take days because if you do it *too* fast the worm will break. And die. And rot. So then the patient dies – from massive and agonizing blood poisoning all through his, or her, body . . ."

By this time the phone line had cleared so much I could hear Andy chuckling.

"Gotcha!" he said, sounding now as if he was in the same room with me. "God had a purpose for everything he made, right? *This* must be why he made the guinea worm."

---

Having committed myself to writing a book about my regiment, I suggested to Frances that we spend a couple of months travelling around Europe so I could recapture the feel of the places I would be writing about.

"Ah," she said, "that *would* be hard to take but I could probably manage."

So out came the maps, and a few days later I booked us a flight to England in early May. I also arranged to buy a car for delivery in London so we could drive ourselves to remote places.

When I broke the news of what was afoot to Dudley and Max, I also sent each of them a draft of the boys' book I had been working on, hoping to make my decision to write a war book more palatable.

Max replied noncommittally, but there was no response from Dudley so I wrote him again.

> *Dear Dudley,*            *March 10, 1953*
>
> *The silence from Boston grows oppressive. Damn it, Spring has come! The snows have melted! Polar bears have retreated northward! And Her Majesty's Mails are being delivered regularly. So what about the boys' book? Fran and I will depart May 1 for Italy and France, where we'll be until mid-July so if you contemplate publication of the juvenile this year, any re-writing will have to be done in the hell of a hurry.*
>
> *The contract between myself and the Regiment is final, and I expect to complete their book by next Xmas. It is now well under way. Pretty hard to describe. Not a history in the usual sense; and it won't be fiction. More of an emotional evocation of the lives and deaths of infantry soldiers of all time, with a subjective feel resembling that of* People of the Deer. *It is being written as a trade book, not as a pedantic tome of only accidental interest to the general public.*
>
> *A war novel is gestating side by side with it but won't be in shape for an editor to look at for another 18 months.*
>
> *I miss your sage advice.*
>
> *Cheers.*

This time Dudley replied relatively swiftly with a bludgeoning of the boys' book, including a demand from Little, Brown, backed by Atlantic Press, that I shorten it by a third, increase the ages of the principal characters from early teens to college students, and eliminate even the suggestion that any of my protagonists might be of mixed race.

My reply was hardly politic.

> *Dear D.*
>
> *If you'll pardon my bluntness, what you and Helen James* [the editor of "juvenile" books for Little, Brown] *seem to want is a Grade B Hollywood scenario – a slicked-up version of Cowboys and Eskimos . . . you seem to want the entire book re-written with a complete change of emphasis so the "white" boy becomes a hero who rescues the native from disaster. . . . LB's concept of Awasin as a savage possessed only of a certain primitive cunning and capacity to cope with nature in the raw is absolutely unacceptable. If you and LB want the book re-written along that line, I won't do it. I value my association with Atlantic highly but have absolutely no interest in revising the book along the lines required by LB.*
>
> *F.*

To which I added a postscript designed, I suppose, to soften the impact somewhat.

> *PS. We have acquired a telephone! BOLTON 19-78 is the number if you should ever care to use it, which won't be easy since there are 14 families on the same party line, and the other 13 are enjoying the novelty by day and night. Maybe you can hear the din they make way down south?*

Not surprisingly, Dudley failed to call me.

———

Trans-Canada Airlines' North Star, a refurbished, prop-driven, wartime DC-4, departed from Malton airport north of Toronto in a drizzle on the first day of May.

Fran and I unabashedly held hands as we stared uneasily out the small porthole into the swirling murk. As the aircraft lumbered along at seventeen thousand feet, we were given trays of chicken salad and tomato aspic, which we had to balance precariously on pillows held on our laps, but we did have real silver, linen napkins, and crystal wine glasses.

The wine did Fran a lot of good.

"If we have to go down in flames," she said, with a sidelong glance out the porthole at the red-hot exhaust belching from the nearest Merlin engine, "at least we'll go in style."

We descended into Goose Bay, Labrador, an hour before dusk, landing at a nominally Canadian, but effectively American, air force base. While the plane was being refuelled, we were herded into a bleak hangar by a U.S. armed escort. The task of our slouching and slovenly G.I. guards presumably was to prevent the Russian spies amongst us from taking pictures of Sabre jets and a score or more B-52 bombers parked in the dim distance.

Darkness had fallen before we took off for the ten-hour voyage across the ocean. Our seats were beside the starboard wing, and one of the Rolls-Royce Merlins seemed only an arm's length away, spitting a long stream of blue flame. The bellowing thunder kept us from sleep. We squirmed fearfully in our seats the long night through, and got no good of it.

The morning of a sunny spring day had dawned when we made a lazy swing over the green islands of Arran and Kintyre before descending into a Royal Air Force base at Prestwick. There were no armed guards here – only a family of young jackdaws perched on a roof ridge, nerving themselves for first flight. Whenever an aircraft roared off the runway, they would teeter forward yearningly then, at the last moment, lose their nerve and scrabble back up the ridgepole.

Airborne again, we flew south at low altitude, avidly taking in the sights. Great numbers of small, round ponds scattered in fields and woods near Liverpool piqued Fran's curiosity. What could they be?

"Bomb craters," I explained. "German bombs which missed Liverpool or were jettisoned by Jerry pilots anxious to head for home. Look at them now! Pretty little frog ponds for cows to drink out of and kids to paddle in."

And so to London, which had become a madhouse as it prepared itself for the coronation of Queen Elizabeth II. The city was so heavily be-draped and bedecked with webs of scaffolding, miles of bunting, and forests of flags that we could hardly get a peek at her face.

If not much else was visible, St. Paul's was still able to float its dome above the tinsel. I flagged a cab to take us there. When the driver heard I had been in London during the Blitz, he volunteered a guided tour of the bombed-out and un-reconstructed wastelands behind the cathedral. The spectacle of those endless blocks of rubble was a stunner for Frances.

"I could never have believed the bombing was that bad. How did anyone survive?"

"Few would have if the Nazis had been able to do what they intended. The idea was to blow and burn London right off the map. Show us what Total War really meant. Knock Britain to her knees. Only the RAF's guts and Goering's stupidities prevented the whole city being reduced to slag."

"Aye," said our driver, "they bastards would have buried us. And yet there's folks thinks we ought to feel guilty-like for what we done to German cities when we got the upper hand. Guilty!" he spat out the cab window. "Cor! When I hears that from a fare, I brings him here, for a look-see whether he likes or no."

We toured the cathedral. Then it was time for a pint and a sausage roll in a nearby pub before tackling the Tower, which was high on Fran's obligatory list. It seethed with visitors. We walked the old stones, viewing jewels, Cockneys, cannon, Beefeaters, dungeons, Bostonians, old armour, Torontonians, et al., until I'd had a surfeit.

My attention strayed to the Tower ravens. One old fellow standing in the middle of a bit of greensward was amusing himself by playing the tourist. He would peer incredulously at some fragment of brick or stone then shriek astonishment to a circle of fellow ravens, while casting gleeful looks at passing humans. I tipped him a conspiratorial wink.

I lay awake for a while that night thinking about the Tower ravens; the myriad coots, ducks, geese, and swans on the park ponds; the house sparrows, starlings, and pigeons in the squares; and something else our taxi driver had told us about. Foxes, stoats, weasels, hedgehogs, rabbits, and pheasants were all colonizing the urban wastelands produced by the bombing. "It's old Mother Nature taking back her own," he'd said. Nurturing that consoling thought, I drifted off to sleep.

On Monday morning we took delivery of a spanking-new, claret-coloured Hillman Minx convertible, which we named Elizabeth in honour of the young queen. Liz was the first car (Lulu Belle excepted) I had ever owned, and very sporty she looked as we made our way out of London into Kent, where the smoke of the city soon gave way to a translucent haze of sea air drifting inland from the distant Channel.

Reaching Dover, we booked into the Hôtel de France, which, unfortunately, had been spared destruction by the German siege guns across the Channel on Cap Gris Nez. The food was abominable; the service surly; the bedding damp; and relays of motorcyclists staged impromptu races around the block throughout the night. At dawn the gulls took over, perching on our window ledge to scream lewd comments and maledictions at us.

Next morning at the Western Docks we watched fearfully as our pretty little car was seized by a gantry crane, swung high into the sky, and dropped into the ferry's hold. The vessel sailed in heavy fog, which lifted as we approached France at Gris Nez. We stared in awe at the monolithic gun emplacements from which the Germans had shelled England. They looked ready to let loose another broadside at any instant, but their day was done. Even before war's end, they had been outmoded by launching ramps from which flying bombs and V-2 rockets were lobbed at London.

Once ashore, we headed south toward the distant Mediterranean, stopping for a night at Avalon, an ancient place perched on a granite outcrop overlooking a tributary of the Seine. The town was in the throes of a huge party honouring the Maquis – guerrilla fighters in the recent war who, despite the abject surrender of their country by Petain, had persisted in a long and bloody struggle against the Nazi invaders.

As Fran and I made our way down one of the steep and crowded streets toward the heart of the town, we were accosted by a hatchet-featured man wearing the distinctive beret of the Maquis. He introduced himself as Georges Roussel and forthrightly asked what we were up to. When I explained that I was a Canadian army veteran retracing my wartime travels, he kissed both of us fervently then slapped his beret on *my* head.

"But how wonderful! We are comrades, *non*? You and your *petite* must help celebrate beating the bastardly Boche!"

He brooked no argument. Taking us one on either arm, he guided us into the crowd, stopping here and there to introduce us to his many friends. It was as if we had been born in Avalon and had returned there after a long absence. Nothing was too good for us. We visited so many cafés and drank so many toasts that we lost count of everything, including time. I remember marching behind brass bands in the blue-clad ranks of Resistance fighters, being dazzled by fireworks, and – vaguely – being escorted back to our hotel by a crowd singing "Auprès de ma Blonde" at the tops of their voices.

We were seriously tempted to stay a while in Avalon for I had a great interest in the Resistance fighters and wanted to learn more about them, but I was impelled to reach the scene of our own battles as soon as possible. So we slipped out of Avalon next morning, bound south for Italy down the old Route Napoléon.

Reaching the shore of the Middle Sea, we drove east to Menton, where a charming Italian customs officer welcomed us to his country. The temptation to linger in one of the many little villages on the Italian Riviera was great, but since we still had many miles to go we pushed on to Milan, then eastward along the broad Po Valley. A few miles beyond Bologna, we turned off the main highway onto a dirt track where, in 1944, the German army had stopped the northward advance of First Canadian Division.

I was on familiar ground.

Crossing the Senio River, we came to Bagnacavallo, in whose ruined houses my companions and I had sought shelter from shells, freezing rain, and the imminence of death during Christmas week of 1944.

A small hotel overlooked the central square. We parked Liz and pushed aside the beaded fly curtains of the ground-floor *ristorante* to enter a dark and cavernous room that was marvellously cool and silent except for the buzzing of a bluebottle. An old man emerged from a back room to serve us sticky glasses of Marsala.

"You seem really far away," Fran murmured to me as we sipped the strong sweet wine.

"I've been in this room before, and slept upstairs," I said, "only then the whole front wall had been smashed open and we parked our jeep in here. One night a shell came through the roof, failed to explode, and bounced down two flights of stairs to whomp into the driver's seat, where we found it next morning, harmless as a sleeping cat."

It may have been the Marsala, or perhaps the white heat shimmering off the walls of Bagnacavallo. Or it may have been the odour of urine, wine lees, cooking oil, and dust – the "burnt umber" smell of small Italian towns. Whatever. The floodgates of memory were swinging open, releasing a deluge of recollections.

Winter is not the season to fight battles on the Adriatic coast of Italy. We Canadians had learned this the hard way during the winter of 1943. The high command, however, either had not learned the lesson or in 1944 deliberately chose to ignore it.

As December approached, First Canadian Corps was ordered to "burst out" of the narrow corridor of coastal plain lying between the mountains and the Adriatic Sea, then sweep north past the coastal city of Ravenna and open the way for a triumphant advance by the rest of British Eighth Army into the Po Valley and northern Italy. The staff officers at Allied Forces Headquarters who contrived this grandiose plan and cheerfully code-named it Operation Chuckle had decreed that we Canadians would have the honour of making the breakout.

We were ordered to begin by attacking across three major rivers, several canals, and innumerable drainage ditches all running between high and steep embankments from the mountains to the sea. All were in spate, and their waters – mountain torrents – were bitterly cold. Each was defended by elite German troops well dug in and well armed.

Chuckle began December 2. The following day the Hastings and Prince Edward Regiment tried to force a crossing of the high-banked Lamone River. The weather was atrocious. Rain, sleet, and snow were turning the coastal plains into a half-frozen quagmire. Nevertheless, as darkness fell on December 3, Baker and Charlie, the two assault companies, began sloshing their way over a flooded landscape toward the start line, which was the base of the southern dyke containing the raging Lamone.

Ten minutes before midnight, our saturated soldiers reached the dyke and flung themselves down on sodden ground to snatch what rest they could before zero hour sent them scrambling up the slope and over the top. The minutes swiftly passed, until suddenly the night exploded with sullen thunder as our artillery fired the opening rounds of a great barrage intended to keep the German defenders deep in their dugouts and slit trenches until the Canadian infantry was on top of them.

Captain Cliff Broad, Baker Company's commander and my close friend, was lying just below the crest of the near dyke when our barrage began. He flattened himself to earth at the wail of approaching shells, which, instead of exploding amongst the enemy, came thundering down on Baker and Charlie companies. The earth shook and heaved. Red and yellow flashes illuminated the charnel scene as shrapnel sliced through steel helmets, bones, and flesh. A biting white smoke added its special horror as phosphorous grenades hanging from men's belts were hit by shrapnel and exploded, immolating those who carried them.

The barrage ceased, and for a moment the living lay in the awful silence of the aftermath, immobile, stunned. Then the cries of the wounded began – a threnody of agony. Half the men of Baker were dead or wounded. Charlie, which had gone into battle with a strength of only two platoons, was now reduced to less than one.

The regiment should have been immediately withdrawn. Instead, it was told to carry on as planned, and the remaining two infantry companies – Able and Dog – were ordered forward. They plodded up through a false dawn that provided just enough light to avoid trampling their dead comrades scattered below the dykes and somehow managed to scramble across the river, scale the far bank, and dig themselves in while enduring a ferocious enemy counterattack.

Reinforcements were desperately needed, but none were available. Cliff Broad took the forty or so survivors of his company across the Lamone and into an attack that drove the Germans back some three hundred yards. Then Baker's men were forced to go to ground in the middle of a vineyard by a hail of mortar bombs and small-arms' fire. Enemy tanks began to converge upon them. Nevertheless, they held until it was all too obvious that to remain where they were would be to die where they were.

Broad gave the order to get out.

Dragging some of the wounded and under intense fire, the survivors scuttled back to the river. Some drowned during the crossing. The remainder, joined now by what was left of Able and Dog, tumbled over the crest of the southern dyke and rolled heavily down its slope. Now they were back at the start line where, nine hours earlier, they had suffered a holocaust from our own guns.

For five days the weather drew a shroud over the Lamone killing grounds. Rain beat down unceasingly. The soil became so saturated that slit trenches filled almost as soon as they were dug. Wet snow plashed a wasteland that had once been neatly patterned vineyards and fields. The only shelter to be found was in a few stone-built farm buildings, which were being methodically pulverized by German guns.

Relationships between us and the remaining civilians grew closer. Since we shared a world of destruction, we began to share other things. Cans of bully beef found their way into the pots of pasta that nurtured *paesani italiani* and *soldati canadesi* alike. An old woman mixed hot wine with the juice of a few scrofulous oranges to put heart into patrols that had to feel their way into the black, bullet-studded nights.

On December 10 the regiment returned to action in Eighth Army's final attempt to justify Operation Chuckle by breaking out of the sodden coastal strip into the open reaches of the Po Valley. By the 12th our forward companies had overrun the German positions on the Canale Vecchio and the Canale Naviglio and were pushing on. Baker Company had the farthest to go. Its objective, a cluster of farm buildings called San Carlo, lay a thousand yards beyond the Naviglio. Charlie, in a supporting role, squelched forward to the sparse shelter of a ditch halfway between the Canale and San Carlo, then dug itself in. Able struck out along a lateral track and was soon fighting desperately for possession of a few scattered houses. What remained of Dog Company was in reserve at battalion headquarters, a shattered farmhouse between the Vecchio and the Naviglio.

By dawn next day, Baker had taken San Carlo and was being counterattacked by at least a battalion of infantry supported by tanks and mobile artillery. At this juncture, our commanding officer, Lt. Col. Donald Cameron, hunched over his radio set, heard a static-filled message from Baker.

". . . attack by heavy tanks . . . look like Panthers . . . lots of infantry . . . ammo almost gone . . . without tank support we'll soon be goners too . . . you want us to hang on or try to pull out? . . ."

The message ended in a burst of static.

The decision Cameron had to make was of the kind that ages men and withers their souls. He *could* not sanction a withdrawal. Too much depended on this bridgehead being held until reinforcements, and especially tanks and anti-tank guns, could reach us.

Holding the microphone close to his mouth, he slowly and distinctly repeated the words: "*You must remain . . . You must remain . . . Our tanks are coming . . . You must remain . . .*"

He paused – but there was no reply. Baker's radio was off the air.

Mired in frigid mud, the men of Charlie Company watched helplessly as the Germans closed in on San Carlo. They watched as Mark IV and Panther tanks methodically shattered each building, reducing each in turn to smoking rubble.

Meanwhile, Able, in houses along the dyke wall, was under attack from two self-propelled guns and a strong force of infantry. Cut off from one another, two of Able's three depleted platoons fled back across the canal, leaving only Nine platoon, reduced now to fewer than a dozen men, to hold the position.

Then it was Charlie's turn. With the leisureliness of those who are assured of victory, the Germans turned on Charlie. The men of its Thirteen Platoon raised their heads during a lull in the bombardment to find themselves staring into the muzzles of a score of German rifles and carbines. Thirteen Platoon vanished and was not heard from again.

The CO did what he could. What remained of Dog Company was ordered forward but, suffering from the effects of seven days of shell-fire and the loss of most of its officers and NCOs, it had also lost heart. Three times it set out for the canal, and three times turned away from the gates of Hell.

Here is Padre Freddy Goforth's description of the scene at battalion headquarters.

"From dawn until late afternoon the house was under constant bombardment – moaning Minnies, 88s, everything in the book came at us. Early on, a shed on the south side was demolished by a direct hit. There were a lot of casks of *vino* in the shed and a number of men had bedded down amongst them and were trying to rest. The casks were all perforated but most of the men miraculously escaped and ran into the main building, soaked in wine. The wine flowed across the floor behind them and for the rest of the day we lived in the sour stink of *vino* fumes.

"As time passed the place grew more and more crowded. The remnants of Able Company found shelter here, along with those of Dog Company. By this time the battle had begun to look like Armageddon for us. Only Charlie was left in front and the messages coming through were increasingly desperate. 'The enemy is pressing close.' 'We're running out of ammo.' 'What are your orders?'

"I would have defied anyone to tell what was passing through Cameron's mind as he quietly told the signaller to reply, 'Help is coming. Hold on.'

"Cameron's coolness steadied us though we were sure the promise of relief was just a pipe dream. With enemy tanks crawling around a few hundred yards in front and capable of crossing the Naviglio, and remembering that behind us were *two* canals that as far as we knew had not yet been bridged and were impassable to *our* tanks, we couldn't see we had much of a hope.

"Suddenly we heard the rumble of tank treads outside. Our common thought was, 'Well, this is goodbye.'

"Then someone peered out a window and yelled 'They're *ours!*' and then we knew how the boys must have felt at the siege of Lucknow so long ago when they heard the skirl of the pipes approaching. Coming up the road toward us was a squadron of British Columbia Dragoon tanks swinging their seventeen-pounder guns from side to side. We heard later that the first of them had crossed the Lamone before the bolts on the bridge were tight."

The Dragoons wasted no time. Finding a ford, the tanks rumbled over the Naviglio, firing as they went. One appeared outside the ruins of the house where a remnant of Charlie Company was making its final stand. As it nosed around the corner of the building, it was hit by a German anti-tank shell. The wounded gunner crawled out of the turret and some of Charlie's men raced out and dragged him under cover. All the gunner said was "Did we make it in time?"

They had made it in time.

Early one afternoon, at an hour when sensible people were letting their dinners digest and avoiding the heat of the day, Fran and I drove along a track beside the Canale Naviglio toward a cluster of white houses glistening in the sun. We drove into a courtyard flanked by spanking-new buildings standing four-square under red-tiled roofs. I thought that if *this* was San Carlo it surely was risen from the grave. I got out and stood uncertainly, waiting for a sign. All was motionless except for a garishly green lizard scampering across a newly laid stone pavement.

Then a door opened and a slim young man came out. He advanced somewhat timidly for, though Fran and I could not know it, we were the first foreigners to come here since the war.

"*Si, signore*," he replied in answer to my question. "This is San Carlo and you and the *signora*" – he smiled at Fran – "are very welcome to Casa Balardini. Please to come in."

We were received in the cool, dark room reserved for ceremony. Roused from their naps by a stentorian cry from Signore Balardini, a big man with straggling moustaches and a belly that gave him presence, the rest of the family came stumbling, running, and striding into the room. Spanning several generations, there seemed no end to them. They clustered around us, touching our shoulders, smiling, laughing, and bombarding us with questions.

Although we were being treated as honoured guests, I was uneasy. How were these people going to react when they realized I was one of the *soldati canadesi* whose guns had contributed to the wartime devastation of San Carlo?

I need not have worried. A middle-aged man thrust a glass of wine into my hand.

"*Canadese, no*? I am captured by you boys in Sicily in 1943. I work for your engineers. They put me in *canadese* uniform and I learn to speak English good. *Canadese molto bene!*"

Relieved, I explained why we were here. Far from souring the mood, this seemed to warm it even more. However, if the Balardinis harboured no resentment toward Canadians, their feelings toward the *tedeschi* (barbarians – as most Italians called the Germans) were another matter.

"When you kick the goddamned *tedeschi* out of here that time, everything gets smashed. Too bad! But don't matter so long you got those Nazi bastards out. We can fix everything so long we are free from those sons of bitching fascists!"

The sentiments of this fervent little speech, repeated in Italian, were vehemently echoed by the family, who now seemed intent on making us one of them.

Frances, who had edged to the door to get some breathing space, was now frantically waving at me. "They're taking the luggage out of the car!" she cried.

They were indeed, having apparently decided we were moving in to Casa Balardini. Only with great difficulty was I able to convince the family we could not stay. There was, however, no gainsaying their demand that we must eat with them before travelling on.

While the women rushed off to prepare the meal, men and children proudly escorted us around the farm. It embraced just three hectares – about seven acres – and everything that had stood or grown on this small piece of earth had been obliterated during the winter of 1944. Now the land had come alive again. Grapes were forming on neat rows of vines. Young orchards were thriving as peaches and cherries ripened. One supple lad swarmed up a tree and showered us with firm-fleshed fruit.

Every inch of soil was in use. Corn grew between the vines and in the aisles between fruit trees. Cabbages, tomatoes, eggplants, and other vegetables flourished between the rows of corn. Narrow strips of wheat crowded to the very edge of the road. There were no weeds on the Balardini farm – there was no room for them. Cows, mules, pigs, goats, chickens, and ducks lived in and around the outbuildings. The place was a living supermarket – as it had to be in order to feed so many human mouths.

Late that afternoon, we sampled its produce. The dishes were too many to remember but I know we ate chicken and kid with a dozen different vegetables, and filled our plates from countless pasta dishes redolent of herbs, spices, and sharp white cheese. Wine flowed freely.

Not until we had eaten and drunk rather more than our fill did the talk turn to the December day when Operation Chuckle had sent Baker Company to Casa Balardini. What remained of the family, deprived of most of its men by military service and German labour round-ups, had taken refuge in the cellars.

"There were only about thirty *canadesi* here," we were told, "then whole companies of *tedeschi* with many *carri armati* [tanks and self-propelled guns] surrounded the *casa* and blew it to pieces, room by room. The noise was so bad our one remaining pig burst out of its sty and ran right toward a tank, and the *tedeschi* shot it with machine guns. . . . Everything that moved got shot. You could smell blood everywhere. . . . My cousin Maria had turned eight the day before; a big girl but thin because there was so little food. She must have been too hungry to think straight. She had sneaked out to what was left of the vegetable garden. When the shells came she just disappeared. Later we found her feet and one arm. . . . Some of the shells had phosphorus inside them, and when they exploded everything was sprayed with fire. Water wouldn't put it out. My aunt was hit by a piece of that stuff and it burned a hole right into her belly. A Canadian soldier bound it up but she died anyway, screaming and screaming."

As the German assault grew fiercer, the surviving Balardinis huddled in a stinking vault below the cattle stable. Then a salvo of shells brought the roof down and the walls tumbled in. One old man was killed and a young woman suffered a crushed thigh. The cattle were all killed.

After overrunning the ruins of the farm, the Germans herded the few surviving Canadians able to walk (the Balardinis thought there were no more than ten) into captivity but did not discover the Italians in their hole. These survivors emerged two days later to find the destruction so complete they abandoned the place to seek refuge with relatives beyond Bagnacavallo.

"When we did come back," the oldest woman told us, "we found everything broken or gone. The next winter was hard. We lived through it. We went to work. And now" – she gave me a gap-toothed grin – "well, *here we are!*"

It was late when, laden with gifts of wine and fruit, we left San Carlo. I also took with me a souvenir of a different kind – a shell fragment from a heap that had been collected from the fields during recent cultivation, a small part of the harvest of steel we and the Germans had sown.

Beyond San Carlo, we and the highway hugged the coast until we reached the port of Ortona on a headland which since ancient times had dominated the world around until, between us, we and the Germans succeeded in reducing much of this city of twenty thousand people to rubble.

Just beyond its ruins we came upon the Moro River Military Cemetery. Here fourteen hundred men of First Canadian Division rot in incomparably beautiful surroundings overlooking the Adriatic. Amongst them is Major Alex Campbell, once my company commander. Alex, an indomitable mountain of a man, was killed on Christmas Day 1943. His father had died in battle with the Kaiser's Germans on Christmas Day 1916.

Fran and I wandered about the battlefields. One morning we visited an observation post where I had spent some of the most terror-filled hours of my life being sniped at by a German 88 mm gun. Now the farmer who owned the land came over to pass the time of day. He offered us a drink from a straw-covered bottle, but even as I sipped the wine my ears were tautly attuned for the shriek of an incoming shell.

We walked along the now-deserted San Leonardo track which had once been the main highway for an army. Beyond it we came to a gully where Doc McConnell, my batman, had dug me a luxurious foxhole – but had forgotten to take into account the cumulative effect of the almost ceaseless rain, which one night brought it all down on my sleeping head.

I had another memory of this gully.

Early in March, the sun had returned and the shell-churned ground had begun to thaw. One day I came upon an old woman prodding the ground with a brass rod from a bedstead. She had no business being there, for all civilians had been evacuated, or so we thought. I questioned her and found she had spent that ghastly winter hiding in an abandoned German dugout. For company she had had her daughter and granddaughter – both of whom had died before the new year began. For months this old woman had endured the unendurable, emerging only to grub for roots and anything else edible – while waiting for the war to end and the ground to thaw so she could bury her dead.

Originally we had intended to continue south to Sicily, on whose beaches the regiment had landed in July of 1943 as part of the first successful Allied invasion of Europe. However, after Ortona I could no longer stomach the bloody memories, so we turned our backs on war for a time in an attempt to escape the grim moods of battle, and became tourists. Crossing back over the Apennines to western Italy, we gaped at Rome, Naples, Pompeii, Positano, and such places as we became part of the frenetic flow of mostly well-to-do foreigners who were again enjoying themselves "doing Europe."

Two weeks of flitting amongst historic monuments, famous art treasures, and the fleshpots and watering holes celebrated in glossy tourist guides were enough for me. In the last week of May I decided we should return to Britain, where I could refresh memories of the regiment's relatively unbloodied sojourn during the early years of the war.

We turned north and after a long day's journey came to Florence.

In 1944, when I had last been here, the Germans had held the north bank of the river and we the south. Although Florence had been declared an open city the Germans reminded us by firing occasional artillery salvos across the narrow waters that they were not to be trifled with.

One afternoon I had gone looking for a place to establish an observation post from which our artillery could direct counter-battery fire and had come upon a riverside estate behind whose high walls rose the cupola of a *palazzo* that looked as if it might serve my purpose. I walked through the open gates. Attached to the shabby and much-neglected *palazzo* was a large greenhouse, which, instead of flowers, housed a sculptor's studio.

At that moment a shell screamed overhead and crashed into a row of houses beyond the walls of the estate. I thought this might be the ranging shot for a possible barrage. If so, a greenhouse would be a poor place near which to linger. I was about to dash for the shelter of the *palazzo* itself when movement behind the glass caught my eye. A white-haired man, handsome and erect, was working at a plaster bust. Another shell exploded and I dropped on my belly. When I cautiously rose again, the sculptor was still at work, apparently unperturbed.

Curiosity overcame caution, and I found a door and entered. The sculptor, who appeared to be in his seventies, glanced up, laid down his tools, and came toward me.

"Welcome, sir." The vibrant timbre of his voice belied his apparent age. "Will you have some wine?"

As we sat on ornate iron chairs under that precarious roof drinking his wine, I saw that the greenhouse studio was full of plaster casts and draped figures – none of them finished.

"You observe my work is only clay and plaster," he remarked, smiling. "Allow me to explain.

"In my younger years I cast my figures in bronze, but then I came to understand the futility of that. How long could even bronze outlast me? A millennium or two perhaps. A fleeting moment in the torrent of the years. So now I work only in clay and plaster – honest materials of the moment – and I no longer harbour delusions of immortality."

Later, as I walked with him through the greenhouse, an almost-life-size clay bust of a young woman caught my eye. He drew off the wet drapes covering her and she was lovely. Realizing that in a few weeks her clay would dry and crack, and she would disintegrate, I was half-inclined to think the old man mad.

Two days later the Germans took note of the high cupola of the *palazzo* and presumably concluded, as I had done, that it could serve as an observation post. Their guns removed it with Teutonic thoroughness – together with the greenhouse and most of the rest of the *palazzo*. Perhaps the old sculptor escaped. I never knew. That night we moved on to fight another battle.


Frances and I left Florence intending to follow the coast to Marseilles then drive north up the Rhone Valley. But that night when we stopped not far from Genoa, we heard that Sir Edmund Hillary had just scaled Everest. The news set us thinking about mountains – and changed our plans.

"What do you say we skip southern France and go over the St. Bernard Pass into Switzerland instead?" I asked my wife. "That way we'd get a look at Mont Blanc, and maybe the Matterhorn."

"*And* meet the St. Bernard dogs? Let's do it!"

Next day, however, we learned the St. Bernard Pass was snow-bound and closed to all traffic. Moreover, nobody had any idea when it might be open again. We looked at one another and decided to press on anyway.

As we entered the mouth of the Aosta Valley, the mountains began to appear through rifts in the overcast. The clouds were luminous with unseen sunlight. Slabs of wet, green stone in marble quarries along the road glowed eerily. Grape terraces marched up steep slopes until they were lost in the high mists. We climbed higher and the valley narrowed. After a couple of hours it unexpectedly widened again to reveal the city of Aosta.

It was now almost dark, and time for us to roost. The Albergo della Corone e Poste in Aosta's main square looked like our kind of place. Its several ancient buildings surrounded a roughly cobbled inner courtyard where post carriages had once rattled and horses had been stabled. The guest rooms within were panelled in dark woods and dimly lighted by leaded windows.

All was presided over by three brothers in their sixties. Frédéric, the courtly middle brother, showed us where to sign the book. Balding, vivacious Domenico led us to our wainscotted room overlooking the square. The oldest brother, portly and rubicund François, escorted us in to dinner then became our waiter, wine steward, and general factotum.

He served us minestrone, steamed trout, tender little steaks with artichokes, strawberries and cream, fresh apricots and cherries, cheeses, and a variety of local wines. Between times he entertained us with tidbits about the history of the Valle d'Aosta. We were the only guests, so the other brothers joined us for coffee and liqueurs.

Glowing with good food, wine, and company, we went to bed under a feather comforter. The steady rumble of rain on lead-sheathed roofs sounded like a benison.

The rain pelted down all night, the wind whined in the chimney pots, and the barometer plummeted. After a late, luxurious breakfast, I dashed across the square to the regional tourist office. The woman behind the desk shook her head regretfully.

"The St. Bernard passes are still closed, I think, *signore*; but if the telephone is working I will call."

For a long time it produced no response. When it did, the news was not good. Two ploughs, one working from each direction, had failed to cut paths through the snow fields of the Great St. Bernard.

A hurricane was blowing through the Little St. Bernard. Snow and sleet were beating down on both. . . .

She smiled sympathetically and suggested we forget about the mountains for a while.

The Albergo Corone was warm and snug so we settled down to endure the delay in comfort. During breaks in the weather, we walked about the old town, explored the countryside, or sat in the snug drawing room of the hotel while one or other of the brothers regaled us with stories about the Valle.

The brothers were a saga unto themselves. Fleeing religious persecution, their paternal ancestor had come over the Little St. Bernard from France late in the sixteenth century.

"He was a dissenter from the Roman faith who only escaped burning because he had a good horse and good sense," François told us. "He led that horse, or it led him, across the pass in mid-winter. The Valle applauded independent ways so it took in horse and man. They went to work for a hostelry. Both produced big families. In time our family took over this hotel while the progeny of our ancestor's horse carried the mail and hauled coaches from one end of the Valle to the other."

"Yes," added Domenico, "and the offspring of both were all dissenters. They still are." He grinned at his brothers. "We three manage not to agree on anything for very long."

There were no post horses at the hotel now but the equine branch of the family still prospered in the nearby Gran Paradiso National Park, where they earned their living carrying visitors into an alpine wilderness.

The peaks and valleys of the Gran Paradiso were home to some of the last wild wolves in Europe; to the almost equally rare chamois (a sheep-like antelope); and to the ibex, a wild goat that a century ago was abundant all through the Alps but now survives, precariously, only in a few parks.

"All the wild creatures are going," said Frédéric gloomily. "That is man's law. Unless a creature becomes our slave it must go. Even the lammergeyer, that wonder of the skies, must go. That is man's law."

Lammergeyers are enormous birds of prey closely related to eagles. In all of Europe, they still existed *only* in the Gran Paradiso, where at the time of our visit fewer than ten remained. Yet even in the park they were persecuted – for their eggs, which were sold to rich collectors for as much as five thousand dollars each!

One night the weather broke, and in the morning we heard that ploughs had reached the col of the Grand St. Bernard. It was time for us to go. The brothers gathered in the courtyard to wave us off and to give us a farewell present. It was a short-handled shovel.

"Leave it in the hospice at the Pass," Domenico told us. "You may not need it but then again you may."

They gave us another parting gift as well. When we stopped that night, we found six straw-wrapped bottles of their own best wines stowed in Liz's trunk.

Ten minutes after leaving Aosta we were climbing into heavy clouds that dimmed the car lights to a pallid glimmer. The scenery we *should* have seen must have been spectacular. To the right the Matterhorn, and to the left Mont Blanc. We saw nothing. In second gear, sometimes in first, we groped through an impenetrable murk. So it went for an hour, by which time we had climbed six thousand feet.

Then we emerged between two layers of cloud and could see a little way about us. Behind was the steeply inclined trough of the valley, clogged with roiling clouds. Around us was arctic tundra, barren and rocky, leading the eye to the snowy peaks of mountains on a level with us. Ahead was a wall of rock rising, so it seemed, perpendicular to our path but scarred by a road climbing its face in tortuous switchbacks.

We drove on and in places our wheels spun. Water vapour reached the carburetor and the consequent lurchings did nothing to ease the strain of manoeuvring along the ledge. Snowbanks appeared and grew deeper until they hemmed us in, sometimes ten feet deep. Masses of wet snow slid into the ruts and several times we had to halt and dig our way clear. The murk closed in again and brought with it a driving wind laden with sleet that clogged the windshield wipers.

The desolation seemed absolute until we swung around the last hairpin bend of hundreds and there before us was the striped barrier of a customs post. Seldom have I seen a sweeter sight.

Only one man was on duty, a half-frozen youngster who gaped at us from a face blue with chill then quickly raised the barrier to let us by. He was a realist who understood that passports and papers were meaningless up here.

"Go with God!" he cried, and fled back to his hut.

We were now on the col at more than eight thousand feet. A gale from Switzerland drove over the pass into our faces. Liz crawled on until the grey bulk of the hospice of St. Bernard loomed ahead. An unadorned, massive, oblong stone structure several storeys high, it looked more like an enormous barracks than a hospice. It seemed to be abandoned. Nobody came to the heavy door when I pounded on the panels, but it was not locked so we pulled it ajar and went inside. We wandered up and down damp, stone-slabbed corridors, finding no human beings. Finally I summoned the courage to hammer on a heavy bronze bell. The echoes died into silence, and we were about to leave that dark and frigid place when a lay brother appeared. He was dwarfish in stature, hard of hearing, and not pleased to see us.

By this time I wanted only to be safely down from the pass into springtime again, but Fran was adamant about the dogs. They had brought us this far and we were going to see them. Where were they? The lay brother gestured toward the door but declined to be our guide. So we went out into the storm, wondering if we stood a chance of being rescued ourselves if we went over some unseen cliff.

A path marked by a red rope strung on long poles wandered off over the drifts. Sinking knee-deep in wet snow, we followed the markers until we came to a low stone building. The door swung open at my touch but again no human being was there to receive us. Presumably the dogs' guardian was holed up in the monastery with the rest of his tribe of troglodytes.

Several St. Bernard dogs were curled up in too-small pens, noses under tails. With some trepidation, we walked down the corridor between the cages to the pen of a gigantic beast whose name, according to a tag on his cage, was Barry. Barry woke slowly, peered at us from bloodshot eyes, and laboured to his feet. I reached through the bars and scratched his ears. When I desisted, he raised an enormous paw, intimating that I had better scratch some more. I did as he wished, while suggesting that he was a shirker who ought to have been out doing his duty in the storm. He gaped hugely as if to say, "My grandfather might have gone out in weather like this, but those were other days."

We left the icy kennel feeling dispirited, for it was clear that in this new age the magnificent dogs were merely objects for tourists to stare at. Returning to the hospice, we managed after a great deal of difficulty to find another monk. When I explained that I was a writer and interested in the story of the hospice, he led us into a chill vault that served as a museum and left us there.

The museum offered faded collections of plants, badly stuffed birds, stone implements jumbled in confusion, and a moth-eaten *stuffed* St. Bernard dog. In addition, there were a few faded pictures. One was of the original Barry who was credited with having saved the lives of twenty-two travellers caught by blizzards on the pass. For the rest, only empty collars, cracked with age and green with mildew, hung on a damp stone wall.

Although the hospice is said to have been founded around 1050 by a nobleman named Bernard, the signature rescue dogs were not part of the establishment until the mid-seventeenth century when one of the monks saw a mountain dog dig out a pilgrim buried by an avalanche under ten feet of snow. Thereafter the dogs became a fixture of the hospice and, eventually, the principal reason for its far-flung fame.

The gale was growing stronger and the swirling snow changing to sleet as we climbed into Liz, turned up the heater, and began the descent into Switzerland.

The road became slush-filled tracks with a high snowbank on one side and what seemed to be a sheer abyss on the other. I was riding the brakes when a hulking great *bus* emerged out of the murk ahead, coming full-tilt at us.

I could only watch helplessly as we slithered forward, coming to rest nudging bumpers with the monster. The driver, a wild-eyed man, thrust his head out his window. His mouth worked furiously but the wind blew his words away so he rammed his vehicle into reverse and went careening backward down the mountain to disappear into the murk.

I inched forward, expecting to come upon a hole in the slender guardrail through which bus, driver, and passengers had plummeted into eternity. However, we soon came upon the bus, its rear end jammed into the inner wall of snow and its driver imperiously signalling me to pass.

I did this with my outside wheels a foot or two from the lip of the abyss. Fran claimed she heard manic laughter, then the bus was behind us, and we were very much alone again.

Some time later the wind dropped, the murk thinned, the grade eased, and the road became recognizable as such. The sun shone and a picture-book alpine valley opened below us. We passed green meadows where pipits sang as they gaily performed their mating flights amongst herds of plump, surefooted cattle.

As we hurried across France to keep a date with the cross-Channel ferry, I persuaded Fran we should spend our remaining time abroad exploring amongst the antiquities of the British Isles. When we reached London we asked a knowledgeable friend where we might go and he suggested we spend a week or two around Wotton-under-Edge in Gloucestershire.

"You'll find lots of old bones thereabouts," he assured us, "some as go back before old Adam's time; before what our teachers used to call the Dawn of Human History. *And*" – he paused for emphasis – "Wotton's got some of the best cider anyone of *any* age has ever tasted."

Next day we headed Liz toward Gloucester, stopping for a night at an inn on the Thames called the Compleat Angler. Our room overlooked a great weir where, on a misty night in 1942, I had had an argument with a swan while paddling a Canadian birchbark canoe "liberated" from Lady Astor's boathouse. The swan won and I had to swim ashore while the canoe went over the same weir that, a hundred years earlier, had caused much distress to the travellers in Jerome K. Jerome's wonderful book *Three Men in a Boat – Not to Mention the Dog*.

As we continued westward, we came to an old cemetery in which we found the grave of a man who had been laid to rest in 1728 at the age of sixty-three. The tomb carried this inscription:

Here lies the Earl of Suffolk's Fool.
    Men called him Dicky Pearce.
His folly serv'd to make folks laugh,
    When wit and mirth were scarce.
Poor Dick, alas! is dead and gone.

What signifies to cry?
Dickys enough are still behind,
    To laugh at by and by.


We were going back into time, but not nearly far enough or fast enough for me. Fran was for lingering in little places like Upper and Lower Slaughter to see what their cemeteries might reveal, but I hurried us on to Wotton-under-Edge.

Wotton (pronounced Wooton) proved to be a town of four thousand, huddled under the edge of the Cotswold escarpment. When I stopped to ask a policeman the way to the Swan Inn, where we had booked a room, he hopped into the back seat and guided us to it.

As the proprietor of the Swan poured us our first glass of the ambrosial local cider, he also briefed us about Wotton-under-Edge.

"A thousand years ago, Wotton was a thriving little place making its living out of the wool trade. Fairs for cloth-makers, buyers, and wool merchants were held every summer. Lively events, I take it. Around 1200 one got out of hand and the whole village went up in smoke. So Wotton was rebuilt closer to the escarpment where the wind ain't so strong, and they added 'under Edge' to its name.

"Gloucestershire was getting to be a regular holiday camp for the high and mighty by then. Henry the Second came here looking for a bit of fluff and found Fair Rosamond, as he called her, though Jane Clifford was her proper name. Henry built her a love nest that only he had the keys to and he surrounded it with a high-walled maze even he got lost in when he'd had a drop too much. But his wife, Queen Eleanor, had a trick or two of her own. She bribed the builder to show *her* the way in and then she did for poor Rosamond. Made her drink poison.

"Rosamond's gravestone tells the story: *Here Rose the Fair, not Rose the Chaste, reposes. The smell that rises is not the smell of roses.*

"So Henry lost his light-of-love, but Edward the Second lost the lot. In 1326 Edward's French wife, Isabella, and our Lord Berkeley fell in love and set about getting rid of Edward. He was hustled into a dungeon in Berkeley Castle, where, him being a weakly chap, it was thought rough treatment would do him in. Rotten food. Stone floors to sleep on. Spot of torture now and again, though nothing as would leave a mark, mind you. But Edward kept his pecker up until his jailers lost patience and one September night they strapped him to a rack, face down, and poured molten lead into his bottom.

"Lord Berkeley was conveniently out of town at the time. When he got the news, he hurried back here – terribly shocked, of course – and had the bod examined by a bevy of his pet priests. *They* couldn't find a mark on him. Concluded the poor sod had died of natural causes.

"Isabella and Berkeley lived happily ever after . . . which just goes to show . . ." He went off to pull a pint of ale for a customer. When he returned he added this snippet.

"The last wolf in Gloucestershire was killed near Wotton in 1281. Ah . . . the last *natural* wolf, you might say. The two-legged kind was still around. Still is. Fouling the manors and mansions round about. There's those of us would be happier with the four-legged kind. Perhaps you might send us some from Canada?"

We explored the countryside during the days that followed. One morning we drove north to Uley Bury, one of many steep-sided lime-stone peninsulas jutting out from the Cotswold plateau toward the Severn River estuary and the sea.

Standing eight hundred feet above the coastal plain, Uley spur thrusts to the west like the prow of a titanic ship. Its "deck" encompasses some fifty level acres and its exceedingly steep slopes are mossed by what remains of ancient forests. Although it is a natural feature, it has the appearance of a human construct because human beings have been modifying the spur through five millennia and have succeeded in reshaping it into a feature that will testify to human obduracy long after the pyramids of Egypt have crumbled into dust.

The carefully levelled crest has been cut off from the parent plateau by several deep ditches dug across the neck of the spur. Banked-up soil and rock from these massive excavations became ramparts that are still fifteen to twenty feet high. Ditches and ramparts were rendered even more formidable by log walls and rows of sharpened stakes. A narrow elevated pathway across them was defended by earthwork forts, now reduced to shapeless mounds.

This was the *least* of what had been accomplished. The upper slopes of the spur itself had been reshaped into two enormous ditches one above the other, each twenty feet deep, dug between three mighty earthen ramparts. The quantities of earth and stone that had to have been dug and moved in order to produce this colossal works boggled my mind. And it had all been done by hand, probably without even the assistance of draft animals.

The first people to use the Bury seem to have been Neolithic herdsmen who, around 3500 BC, stockaded livestock on the wind-swept crest of the spur behind wooden fences or piles of brush intended to keep the stock in and predators out. For about a thousand years, Stone Age people lived on the crest in spring, summer, and fall, probably descending into the shelter of the forests during hard winters. Then things changed. Mankind made a "great leap forward" by discovering how to smelt and work tin and copper. The Bronze Age had arrived, bringing better tools – and deadlier weapons.

In the troubles that inevitably followed, people began making use of the Bury as a place in which to defend themselves against their own kind. Ditches were dug and banks raised. These protective works remained of modest proportions through a millennium, suggesting that war and the rumours of war were then still of relatively rare occurrence. But around 1000 BC mankind here made another spectacular technological leap by learning to smelt and work iron.

The Iron Age seems to have reached Gloucestershire around 700 BC. In its wake it brought not only deadlier weaponry but invaders from Europe, ones who knew how to wield iron axes, swords, and spears and had no hesitation about doing so. In their desperate attempts to resist these invasions, the people of the Bury (who may never have numbered more than a few hundred) expended almost unimaginable effort improving their fortress and the encircling ditch-and-rampart systems.

By 300 BC the enclosure on the crest had become home to a more-or-less permanently beleaguered people being assailed by a singularly ruthless warrior race from across the Channel: the Celts. True products of the Iron Age, the Celts were fierce conquistadors before whose iron might no Bronze or Stone Age people could long hold out.

The Celts stormed Uley Bur, probably slaughtering the male defenders, seizing their women and cattle, and occupying the lands and habitations.

Although the Celts reaped rich rewards from being at the leading edge of the technology of their times, there was a price to pay. Weapons that can kill an enemy inevitably turn upon those who wield them. The Celts began turning upon each other. They refurbished captured hill fortresses, and built more like them. These became tribal strongholds from which they mounted raids on other Celts. Uley Bury acquired new ditches and ramparts, together with new walls of stone and timber.

The Celts did not remain at the forefront of "civilization." Shortly after the beginning of the Christian era, the Romans invaded England. The Celts resisted furiously but now were militarily outclassed. One by one, their hill forts were assailed by Roman legions equipped with giant catapults and other modern inventions. One by one, the forts were taken and the defenders enslaved or put to the sword.

Thereafter, most of the hill forts, Uley Bury amongst them, stood abandoned.

Fran and I picnicked in the shelter of a gatehouse mound, cat-napped in the pale sunshine, and then explored the Bury.

"Mind you keep your eye peeled for adders," we had been warned. "Little devils'll be out looking for a bit of sun. But not to worry – unless you step or sit on them."

We met no adders but, as we climbed to the highest part of the ramparts, did meet a fox, who gave us a casual wave of his tail.

We looked northwest across the good farmland of the Severn valley and beyond the muddy-hued estuary to the distant Welsh mountains. Snowdon, the highest peak in Britain, was a looming presence on the farthest horizon. To the south, I could see the grey void of the Bristol Channel and the Exmoor hills of Devon. Southeast lay the chalk cliffs of Wiltshire. Bursts of watery sunshine swept over this magnificent panorama, illuminating distant details – a fishing vessel ploughing the estuary; a glitter of wet slate roofs from some village far to the northwest; and fighter jets swarming from an airfield near the smoky sprawl of Bristol.

Close at hand was a tumbledown hut sheathed in galvanized iron. It seemed an inexplicable anomaly in such a place, and later I complained about it as being a desecration.

"An observer corps station during the war," I was told. "Fellows used to perch up there night and day listening and looking for Jerry planes. Did it myself. I was up there one moonlit night Jerry bombed Bristol. A sight I won't forget. Whole damned place looked to be going up in flames. Searchlight beams thick as hedgehog quills. Ack-ack flying about thick as rain. A stick of bombs fell straight across Wotton, blew up half a dozen houses. Towards the end, a Jerry pilot jettisoned a big one that crashed down right into the Bury. Like a bloody earthquake, it was. Scared the lights out of us chaps on watch though it hurt nobody except rabbits.

"Ah, yes, this old Bury has seen some queer sights in its time. And I don't doubt, given the nature of the beast, it'll see some more."

"The beast?" Fran asked.

"The two-legged one, me dear. The two-legged one, don't you know?"

# · 5 ·

## WES'MAKOON

I had gone to Europe in the spring of 1953 principally to gather material for the story of the Hastings and Prince Edward Regiment. That summer and fall I did the same in the regiment's home territories of Hastings County and Prince Edward County, a scant three hours eastward of Albion Township.

Even before the 9th of September, 1939, the day Canada committed herself to the war against fascism, men and youths from the two adjacent counties had begun volunteering for service. By war's end, more than two thousand lumbermen, miners, and bush rangers from Hastings (the northernmost county), together with over a thousand farmers, fishermen, and small-town dwellers from Prince Edward County had served with the regiment. It took one of its nicknames – Plough Jockeys – from the southerners, and the other – Hasty Pees – from the northern county men.

I needed to know more about the peacetime lives and the world that had spawned and nurtured these men. The first of many visits was to the home of Cliff Broad, a close comrade during the Italian campaign and the man who had led Baker Company during the Lamone bloodbath. Late in 1945, Cliff returned to Bancroft, the unofficial capital of north Hastings, where he took over the largest of the town's three garages. It held the General Motors franchise and so was nominally a bastion of capitalism but Broad's Garage operated more like an outpost of socialism. As Cliff put it:

"I wasn't running no goddamn business to make a fortune for myself, or for some Yankee outfit as was already too goddamn big for its britches. I run her to make a *living* for me and a bunch of characters been addled by vino and gunfire."

Broad's Garage provided work for many veterans and helped a lot more by selling them GM vehicles at a discount *not* authorized by the manufacturers. This deviation from proper business principles did not sit well with General Motors' high command.

"Boss man for Canada called me a lousy Commie on the phone," Cliff recalled with unconcealed satisfaction. "So I called *him* a capitalist bloodsucker. And things ain't never been the same between us since."

When I wrote Cliff in the summer of 1953 to tell him I planned a trip to Bancroft, and asked if I might stay with him a day or two, he replied in typically succinct fashion.

> *Dear Squib:*
>
> *Come soon as you like. Stay long as you want. Plenty rum and venison with wild wild women so don't bring nothing with you. Specially not the Clap! Ha ha ha ha!*

I set off in Lulu Belle, which seemed appropriate since she was of army ancestry and tough enough to be at home in a once-bustling mining and lumbering region even though, to quote Cliff, it was one that had been "pretty near mined out, lumbered off, and generally fucked up."

Cliff was not at his garage when I arrived but a mechanic, whom I recognized as a survivor of the regiment's mortar platoon, obligingly called his boss's home and got his wife on the phone.

"Etta Mae says for you to stay put and they'll come and git you afore you can say shit!"

A few minutes later, a battered pickup screeched to a halt and out spilled Cliff and his pint-sized wife. He was waving a bottle of rum and she, an empty pint jar.

"*Fill'er up, you old son of a bitch!*" roared Cliff as Etta Mae thrust the jar into my hands. "You got catchin' up to do! They's a bunch waitin' for you up to the house right now . . . and they ain't whistlin' Dixie!"

I tailed the pickup to a nondescript bungalow on the edge of the sprawling little town, then followed the Broads into their front parlour – which was ankle-deep in week-old chicks.

"*Watch your feet, goddamn it!*" Cliff bellowed. "You step on one of them puffballs and Etta Mae'll be up and down your back like a Tiger tank!"

With this he shoved me into a kitchen full of squalling people (every one of whom seemed to have a glass or mug in hand) and into the arms of a squat, demonic-looking woman who held a glass in *each* of her hands.

"*Nelly B!*" Cliff bawled in my ear. "*Watch out for her! Got the kick of a high-octane mule!*"

And, he might have added, the tongue and disposition of an alley cat. Nelly B did not approve of my beard. With a penetrating scream she promptly categorized it as belonging to the "*wrong end of a fucking porcupine! Back off! It makes my poor ass ache!*"

I was not prepared for a Bancroft party, which typically began in mid-morning and could continue for several days. Consequently

I was much relieved when Cliff steered me out of the milling mob of people and chickens for an introductory tour of the town.

Our first stop was Bancroft's sole legal "liquor outlet." It was owned by the Ontario government but managed by Bogey Alexander, who had been our regimental quartermaster in Italy. Bogey presented me with a 48-ounce bottle of Lemon Hart Demerara Rum and, when I tried to pay for it, barked almost savagely:

"Bloody well not! Least the fucking government can do for a guy's been fighting for King and Country the last few years is *give* him a good bottle of booze when he comes home! Here now, have another! Don't want the one you got to feel lonely!"

Cliff and I spent most of that afternoon drifting around town, frequently stopping to share Bogey's largesse with passers-by. One of these was a police constable who had been a lance corporal in my platoon until part of a foot was blown off by a land mine during the invasion of Sicily. He joined us in the cab of the pickup and helped himself generously to the Lemon Hart.

"Well, shit a brick, *Mister* Mowat. I figured you wasn't worth the powder to blow you to hell when you was our platoon lieutenant . . . downy-faced kid as didn't know his ass from a hole in the ground! Like to get us all killed, only most of us made it through so I guess I can call you Squib now, eh? Anyhow, you're no problem now. No sons-a-bitchin' Jerries gunning for us now. Safe as farts in a sewer now."

Safe from German soldiers, but there were other dangers. By the time Cliff got us back to his house, I was so far out of it that Etta Mae made me rest on a cot in the cellar, with a hound bitch nursing a litter of pups under my bed.

Dawn found me asleep in Lulu Belle, parked squarely in the middle of Bancroft's main street.

Although the hour was early, traffic was already heavy; mostly overladen logging trucks whose drivers were not amused to find us blocking the right-of-way. Some steered their behemoths so close to the jeep they set it rocking like a canoe in a tide rip. After a couple of such close encounters, I abandoned Lulu Belle for the relative safety of the Broads' bungalow, where I found Cliff and Etta Mae breakfasting on rum and coffee, oblivious to the welter of chicks, dogs, and party debris surrounding them.

I feared there would be repercussions from my road-blocking escapade but Cliff poured me an eye-opener and reassured me.

"Don't fret none, Squib. I'm Bancroft's police commissioner, and *you* are a *guest* of this goddamn town. The boys will bring your jeep back to you good as new."

Nevertheless, he may have concluded this would be a good time to exchange the urban for a rural milieu and to introduce me to the world of his forefathers – principal amongst whom was Harv Gunter.

"Harv was my granddaddy on my mother's side. No more'n five foot six, he was the *biggest* man ever lived hereabouts. His left eye – 'my leetle eye,' he called it – was a good bit smaller than the other, which give him a look would make you think twice about crossing him. Could lick his weight in wildcats but never had to do much scrapping. All he had to do was squint at a fellow and maybe open and close his two fists, as was as big as hams off a bull moose.

"Although Harv wasn't a fellow to throw his weight around, he was as good as king of Wes'makoon, which is what we call most of north Hastings. The Indians as lived here before hell boiled over and the palefaces arrived called it something in their own lingo that sounded like West-al-macaroon, after a big lake in the middle of it. But their name got whittled down, same as the timber as used to cover the country like hair on a bobcat got shaved off.

"Harv's granddaddy, Ananias Gunter [Gunther], was a soldier of fortune with a Hessian regiment as helped chase the Yankees south when they invaded Canada round about 1812. After that little ruckus was over, Ananias and some of his buddies figured not to go home to the Old Country in Germany where dukes and earls and suchlike owned pretty much everything, so the British discharged them here and they started making a living.

"Ananias joined a logging crew working the Ottawa River. Pretty soon he tied up with a spry young Algonquin squaw who took her pale-face up the Madawaska to Wes'makoon Lake, where her people lived.

"Ananias liked the gal, the country, and the folk so much he settled himself down right there. And passed the word to some of his old chums to come and join him. Which some of them did. One was an ex-Limey grenadier named Broad, and he was no slouch at start-ing a family hisself. . . .

"But what the hell! You don't want to listen to me blowing off about Wes'makoon when you can look it over for yourself. Throw what you need into the back of my truck and we'll be on our way."

We drove south out of Bancroft for half an hour before turning east-ward along a dirt road into the hinterland. At first sight, Harv Gunter's world seemed unprepossessing: lumbered off, burned over, and scarred by mining forays. However, life had not abandoned it. Larch, birch, poplar, and spruce saplings were hard at work masking the destruction and healing the wounds. Innumerable clear little streams, which we gingerly crossed on shaky wooden bridges, were full of trout. The streams invited us to stop and test the palatability of their water mixed with white lightning (moonshine) from a screw-top can labelled *Emergency*, an integral piece of equipment aboard Cliff's truck because, as he put it, "you never knows when the devil might come calling."

We saw no other people until we reached Gilmour, once a settle-ment of lumberjacks, now reduced to little more than a dusty cross-roads and a weathered general store owned by Lorne McAllister, an ex-Hasty P who had taken a bullet in the belly during the battle to liberate Rome.

Lorne pronounced our emergency rations to be "near as fucking wicked as I-tie vino," before sending us on our way with a warning to watch out for a black bear he had raised from a cub but that had now gone off on its own and was making its living catching trout from bridges and culverts along the road.

"Crazy bugger thinks he owns them places! Lays with his arse humped up right in the middle of the road, lookin' down into the water ready to take a swipe at any trout swims close.

"Best you wait 'til he sees fit to let you by. Been known to take a swipe at a car if you interrupt his fishing. Name is Bert . . . in case you want to try talkin' your way past."

Beyond Gilmour we were in moraine country where the last great glaciation had deposited a network of sandy eskers and gravel drumlins on the unyielding granite. This had provided hospitable ground for trees, moose, deer, beaver, eagles, and suchlike but the soil was too poor for cultivated crops. Nevertheless, we passed the occasional clearing. Cliff identified these as having once been "farms."

As the hot afternoon drew on, we came to an area of ancient bog surrounded by a few hundred acres of something resembling arable soil. Fields had been laboriously carved into its surface and their outlines were still preserved by remnants of snake-rail fences. Nearby was what had once been a village of log and frame houses. The doors and windows of most gaped wide and I saw no living beings, not even a dog, on the deeply rutted street.

"This here's what's left of Gunter," Cliff explained. "Where them as favoured farming tried their hands. Harv weren't one of them!"

He gestured contemptuously out the truck window.

"*Real* Gunters, and the Broads and their like, was *woodsmen* – not plough jockeys! Lived offen the land the way God made her. Did a bit of lumbering, log-driving, and furring enough to get what little cash they needed. And they lived the hell of a lot better, *and* longer, than them poor damn groundhogs in Gunter trying to raise cattle beasts and garden truck."

The road ended a few miles farther on at a small clearing on the southern end of what the map calls Westlemkoon Lake. Cliff drove right to the shore, where a heavy-bodied skiff was moored to a rickety pole wharf. Turning off the truck's engine, he reached behind him and pulled out a virginal bottle of Demerara rum which he uncorked with his teeth before handing it to me.

"We're nearly home, me lad. This here's the *Queen Mary*, oldest boat on the lake and queen of them all. She'll take us the rest of the way. Have a swig."

The lake's southern arm did not seem particularly remarkable to me. Surrounded by low-lying land, the water was shoal, boggy, and full of small brush-covered islands appearing to be nearly awash.

"Not your tourist country, thanks be!" Cliff commented as he gassed up *Queen Mary*'s pre-war outboard. "*Moose* country, and deer and bear. If it's pretty scenery you wants, you got to go to the north end. But if it's a full belly, peace of mind, and company as feels the way you do, this here's as good as pushing through the Pearly Gates!"

I was curious about our hulking, flat-bottomed, square-ended scow. Cliff explained that she had been built by his father, Will, at the time Queen Mary was newly come to the throne.

"Will was a dab hand with wood. Give him an axe, a swede saw, and a bowie knife and he could-a built a yacht *fit* for a queen. He built this one for Harv as he wanted a boat strong enough to haul a moose. Will made him one strong enough to handle an elephant – 'cause you never could tell what Harv would bring home."

The noisy, smelly, single-cylinder Evinrude churned us northward along a western shore presenting an unbroken green palisade of remarkably large trees, some of which may have predated the tree-killing scourge that devastated the New World after the white man's coming. We ran for an hour then Cliff put the helm hard over and we headed toward the forest wall. Less than a hundred feet from it, a water-gate seemed to open before us as the forest briefly swallowed the *Queen*, then spat her out again into a hidden reach stretching far to the westward.

The sun was gone by now, leaving a flamboyant sky flaming over the inky waters of West Reach. The *Queen* lumbered on until we were abeam of the perfect cove – a sensuous curve of stippled sandy beach backed by a natural meadow with mixed woodland beyond, the whole protectively shielded by a curving ridge topped by tall white pines.

Cliff cut the engine and, as we drifted shoreward in the silence of the evening, murmured, "This here's what we call Ananias. It's where that young squaw brought her soldier to meet the folks. It's where he settled down and never after strayed no further than his legs or a canoe could carry him. That big old house up there" – he pointed – "that's where Harv was born."

Harv Gunter's birthplace was a massive, single-storey log structure perched high enough up under the shoulder of a protecting ridge to have a commanding view of the long reach below it. Built of ten-inch square logs fitted so closely they hardly needed caulking, it was fronted by an elevated porch from which a watcher could keep tabs on any sizeable moving thing for miles around.

"One time this was an Algonquin village," Cliff explained. "Back of that meadow is where they buried their people, no matter how far away they had to bring them. Ananias is likely there, though there's no marker to say as much."

"Is Harv Gunter buried there too?"

Cliff snorted. "Well now, them goody two-shoes in town will tell you he's under the sod in the churchyard. Some of us thinks different. If there's a coffin with his name onto it in the churchyard I doubt he's in it. But let's get us on up to his house."

The split-log front door had no lock nor was it fitted with an inside drawbar. Anyone could enter as readily as we did simply by lifting a latch made from deer antler.

The spacious living room was strewn with faded, handmade woollen mats and furnished with tables, chairs, and a pair of couches ingeniously constructed of cedar billets. A stone fireplace designed to consume four-foot logs dominated the western wall. Above it hung a battered brass bugle. An ancient seven-day clock ticked noisily from the centre of the mantle. I wondered who kept it wound.

"Nobody as I knows of" was Cliff's short response to my query.

I was surprised there were no trophies of the hunt on the log walls.

"Harv wouldn't abide such," Cliff explained. "Claimed nailing up skins and head bones of wild creatures for decoration wasn't no better than nailing up the skins or skeletons of people."

He paused to fill a mug with rum before adding, "Come out onto the deck. Something I got to do."

A gleaming quarter moon was rising as he led the way outside, mug in one hand and the old bugle from above the fireplace in the other. Then, standing silhouetted against the pale sliver of moon, he tossed the drink of rum as far into the darkness as he could, paused a moment, then raised the bugle to his lips and blew a long and vibrant blast across the black waters of the reach.

Echoes blared back and forth around us, seeming to imbue the now almost invisible world with an unearthly sentience. Cliff lowered the bugle and turned toward me.

"Payin' compliments, as the navy fellows say. This here's Harv's place, and this here old army bugle belonged to Ananias. Least we can do is pay *our* compliments to the both of them."

My curiosity about the man who had last lived in this house had been mounting all day. I questioned Cliff about him now, but Cliff had become taciturn – or was somewhere else perhaps – and answered shortly or not at all. I did learn that Harv had been born in 1870 or 1871 and that his mother, who was part or largely Algonquian, had died when he was young.

By 1890 or thereabouts, he had become a skilled "river dancer" on the Madawaska and Ottawa rivers, floating timber to the mills downstream. He had enlisted at the outbreak of the First Great War and was soon sent overseas where he seems to have been a trial to both sides, so successful at killing Germans that he was promoted several times, only to be demoted again because of his disdain for authority. According to Cliff, Harv had been recommended for medals but had never accepted one because he held that "killing a man or a beast amounts to about the same thing. Times, it *has* to be done, but it ain't ever nothin' to brag about."

By 1920 he was back in his own country, married and determined never to leave again.

The night grew chilly, but the heat from the birch billets we thrust into the cast-iron cookstove took care of that. A golden glow from the tall glass chimneys of several oil lamps contributed its own warmth as Cliff busied himself frying venison fillets and I pan-baked a bannock, as I had learned to do in the far north.

I slept in perfect peace that night.

Next morning, after a swim and a breakfast of cornmeal porridge with canned milk and brown sugar, Cliff took me out on the lake. The *Queen* bore us sedately northward across broad openings, between rocky islands, and past deeply indented bays through a land whose ravaged forests were labouring in rebirth. Cliff kept the old girl throttled down, explaining, "If I opens her up she don't go any faster – just pushes half the lake ahead of her and tows the other half behind. Slow and steady is her bestest way."

It was the proper way. We disturbed nobody and no thing. Ospreys fishing for *their* breakfasts hovered near at hand. A pair of ravens laboured out from shore to gawk and mumble derisively. Loons surfaced alongside like tiny submarines emerging from the deeps, and their haunting halloos pierced the blather made by the old Evinrude like knives thrust through butter.

Air and water were alive but we encountered no other people until Cliff steered the *Queen* into a labyrinth of serpentine channels and we sighted a low structure snugged into a tiny cove. It was so unobtrusive that at first I mistook it for a beaver house, but it assumed human proportions as we approached. An elderly man sporting a dishevelled shock of white hair stepped out of it, peered at us, then imperiously gestured for us to come ashore.

We did so to be warmly greeted by eighty-seven-year-old Lawrence Gunter, Harv Gunter's first cousin. Long a widower, Lawrence lived alone, though he currently was enjoying a visit from his middle-aged daughter, Clary, lithesome, good looking, and hospitable and who had only just paddled back from hauling an illegal gill net set behind the island. She insisted we share a feed of "jumping fresh" lake trout.

Over his first tin plate heaped high with fried trout, Cliff proposed a toast to his uncle Harv.

"Old bugger surely liked his drop," Cliff remembered fondly as he raised his mug. "Weren't a *heavy* drinker, but always partial to a nip. Drank to be sociable, you could say. One time I asked him if he'd ever turned down a drink. He give me a sour look like I'd asked a damn fool question, and says, 'Well, goddamn it, yes I did. Twice. Once I wasn't asked . . . and once I wasn't there.'"

Lawrence laughed as he poured himself another shot and told us of a nearby cove whose flat, limestone shore held a number of barrel-shaped holes drilled by boulders whirled around and around by the downpour from a long-vanished waterfall.

"Some of them rocks as made the holes still lays at the bottom of them so much as six feet down. Indians have a story about that. Say the holes was made by a giant stone-pecker bird lookin' for rock worms big around as a man's arm. Say it was a sacred place, and most white folks got the notion and steered clear of it.

"All except Harv . . . 'cause that's where he used to make his shine!"

Lawrence paused to fill his cup, which he raised in salute to his vanished cousin.

"Best goddamn shine ever hit this country! And he made enough of it could pretty near have floated a run of logs.

"Only a scramble of people ever knowed this was where Harv kept his pot and his still. He'd cook his mash right in them big holes in the rock, and he kept his still in the biggest one. When she was runnin' there'd be this little feather of steam comin' out the hole.

"Harv's secret never got out. We kept it right close in the family, and the Indians was into it with us. But the *shine* got out right enough. It was drunk down in Belleville and Kingston and even so far away as Ottawa. My gawd, she *was* good stuff!"

Many tales were told that day, and Harv Gunter was the subject of most of them.

Clary recalled how he had taught her to hunt bear.

"When I turned ten, he took me out on his trapline. After he was satisfied I could keep up, handle dogs, and shoot pretty straight, he took me bear huntin'.

"Harv never killed but one a year – always a young boar in its prime. Wouldn't never kill sows or cubs nor let any of us do it. Nor he wouldn't kill a bear two years runnin' in the same part of the country. Used to tell us, 'Give the bears a fair shake and they'll do likewise,' was what he said.

"Fall of the year when I was twelve, he took me way to hell and gone back into the country by canoe to get a bear to fill the winter fat barrel. We looked over five or six afore he found the one he wanted – a roly-poly so fat he looked like a big black sausage. Harv dropped him with a shot to the head from his old .44.40.

"Our canoe was not too far away and downhill from where we was so Harv figured to carry Mister Bear down there to skin him out and cut him up on the beach, where everythin' was handy. He was a pretty heavy lift but we strung him upside down from a tamarack pole and off we went with one of us on each end of the pole and Harv leadin' the way.

"Trouble was . . . the damn bear weren't dead! The bullet had creased his skull and knocked him arse over tea kettle but on the way down he started comin' 'round and chompin' his jaws no more'n an arm's length from the seat of Harv's trousers.

"Course I yelled for Harv to stop and shoot the bear again, but we was into a patch of deadfall timber from an old fire and it was heavy goin' and Harv was hot and mad and wouldn't stop.

"'Don't you fret,' he yells over his shoulder. 'Bugger ain't et me yet, and we ain't stoppin' 'cause there's an axe at the beach so there's no need to waste another bullet.'

"We hustled on with the both of us right out at the ends of the pole and it bendin' near double. The bear gettin' more and more uppity, and me yellin' at Harv to stop and shoot it, and him yellin' back, 'Don't you fret! We ain't et yet!'

"We hit the beach at the run, and when we dropped the pole Harv went for the axe and swung on the bear. Took him four or five whacks to kill it dead, and I'll be damned if he didn't say he was sorry while he was at it. Not to *me*! To the *bear*!

"'I has to finish you off the hard way, young feller,' he says kind of sorrowful, "cause I'm not so good a shot as I used to be.'"

Harv Gunter seldom apologized to anyone about anything. After we had all had a little noontime nap and refreshed ourselves with black tea, Lawrence told the story of how Harv had dealt with the first people from "out front" who had the temerity to settle by the lake.

"That were late in the twenties. They'd been a few strangers come to Wes'makoon afore that, mostly hunters or prospectors or the like, but they was fly-by-nights as never stayed for long. Then one of the high-and-mighty Eaton crowd from Toronto got wind of Wes'makoon and come for a look-see at the north end aboard a buckboard on a logging trail – the only road into the lake in those times.

"The fellow liked what he saw so much he decided to build himself a hunting and fishing lodge. He did her up proper! Built a castle of logs and timber grand enough for a prince, which was his style 'cause he owned a department store in Toronto half as big as the whole of Bancroft and had a mail-order business selling everything from ready-cut, build-your-own house kits to fancy women's knickers. Sent out catalogues thick as the Bible of all the stuff they had for sale right across the country. Every family round about had the latest Eaton's catalogue to study over and order out of, and an old one out in the backhouse where it could be put to good use – except the shiny pages which weren't no damn good for nothing.

"Anyways, Eaton built his big place on a point at the north end. He was the lord of creation there for certain . . . but Harv Gunter was still number one on the lake and the country all around and seemed like the Eaton fellow was smart enough to understand that. Sometimes he'd invite Harv into the sawdust castle, as we called it, and give him a drink, though his lordship never touched the stuff hisself. And sometimes Harv, who never liked to be beholden, would guide the Eatons and their guests fishing where the big ones was . . . sort of tit for tat, you might call it.

"Well now, one time his lordship sent a message down to Ananias saying as he wanted five canoes at the Eaton dock at 9:00 a.m. sharp next morning to take a party of important guests out fishing. Harv warn't none too pleased because it sounded too much like an order, and that put his back up. Anyways, he only had two canoes at Ananias and 'twas too late to get more without he'd have to chase all over the lake to find some, so he settled for two canoes and three rowing skiffs.

"We set off with them early enough next morning, but a stiff headwind blew up and slowed us down so we never got to the castle 'til a little after nine. We was tied up there and waiting while one of Eaton's flunkeys went up to the big house to git his master, who come back down with his crowd of bigwigs and all their fishing gear.

"Eaton comes to the edge of the dock and there he stops and gives Harv, who was in one of the canoes, a look black as thunder.

"'Mis-tur-Gun-ter!' he says slow and cold, but loud, 'I believe I ordered *five canoes . . . for nine o'clock*. I only see two and it's twenty minutes past the hour. . . . Can't you *read*, Mister Gunter?'

"I was surprised Harv didn't blow his top, but he just got to his feet real slow, put his hands on his hips steady as a rock, and says as smooth as silk, 'Well now, *Mister* Eaton, I can read good enough out of your goddamn catalogues to pick an order and mail it off. But what happens then Mister Eaton? I waits and I waits, and maybe someday a parcel comes . . . and when I opens her I finds some goddamn thing I never ordered, don't want, and can't use, along with a piece of paper with printing onto it as says, SUBSTITUTED!'

"Harv stopped a while and looked around at all them people listening, before he adds, 'So now then, *Mister* Eaton, how the hell do *you* like *them* apples?' With that he picks up his paddle and leads the whole kit and caboodle of us back down the lake.

"I don't know as them two ever spoke a word to each other after. But that weren't the end of it. Before the Big War one of Eaton's sons took to bringing his family to stay at the castle summertimes. His wife were the real snotty kind who was raisin' their son Georgie to figure he weren't part of the common herd.

"There was still a few lunges [muskellunge, giant members of the pike family] in the lake them times and Georgie's daddy was desperate anxious to catch one. When he found out Harv knowed where some was, he come down to Ananias in his big mahogany speedboat and soft-talked Harv into taking him and Georgie to troll for one some time soon.

"Harv brought the *Queen Mary* up to the castle's dock. He was always fussy about stowing a boat. It had to be done just right. He saw to it every bit of gear was put aboard just so, then put the people to their seats.

"Young George – he might-a been ten or twelve – was the last on the dock. Harv looks up at him standing there and says, pretty mild for him, 'What you waiting for? Damn it, Georgie, git into the boat and sit down nice and quiet 'longside your daddy.'

"Georgie just stood there a bit and then *he* says, '*You* ain't supposed to call me Georgie. *You're* supposed to call me *Master* George.'

"You could'a heard Harv's answer down to the south end of the lake.

"'GIT YOURSELF INTO THE BOAT BEFORE I CALLS YOU SHIT FOR SHORT!'

"Georgie git, and pretty smart about it – but I never heard as Harv had any dealings with the Eatons after."

The day was getting old before we left Lawrence and Clary. Cliff was ready to head for home but even though I knew the Eaton "castle" had mysteriously burned to the ground during the war years, I thought I'd like a look at it and at the north end.

Cliff was not encouraging.

"You won't like it. Different place up there. But we'll go a ways."

We had gone less than a mile farther when we were confronted by a garish, pink-painted cottage perched high on an island from which most of the trees had been cut to provide an all-round view. The cottage and its triple-width boathouse were tightly shuttered and at the end of a floating dock was a sign writ large enough to be read from hundreds of yards away.

WARNING

PRIVATE PROPERTY

KEEP OFF

BY ORDER

W.P.A.

"Who the devil is W.P.A.?" I asked.

"Wes'makoon Protective Association," Cliff snarled, and went on to explain that since the end of the war a flood of strangers from "out front" had followed the Eatons and built summer places around the northern shore of the lake. Now, he told me profanely "the fuckers" were taking steps to ensure that all the inhabitants, old and new, were properly regulated.

"They asks us to their meetings, and sometimes we goes and listens to their foolishness. But we sure and hell don't join their association, and we don't pay no heed to the rules they make, 'less it suits us, which it don't often.

"When they gets too uppity . . . well, then it seems like water worms bores holes in the hulls of their fancy speedboats; molasses gets into their gas tanks; and their new-fangled floating docks come apart even when there ain't no storms. And then," he added with relish, "the bears – leastwise I supposes it's the bears – makes themselves comfortable in them shiny boxes they calls houses. Like them over there."

Cliff was pointing to a whole street of summer cottages coming into view along a piece of shoreline whose trees and bushes had mostly been removed to make room for neat little suburban enclaves.

W.P.A. signs were ubiquitous, but were not the only proclamations of a new regime. As the *Queen Mary* opened the northern arm of the lake I was able to read, from a distance of at least a mile away, glaring letters painted on a granite outcrop:

W BLAKE PITTSBURGH USA

Cliff slowed the outboard to a mutter. "Seen enough?" he asked.

I surrendered. The *Queen* turned about, but Cliff was not through with me yet. Halfway home, he steered to the foot of a high cliff on the eastern shore, near the top of which the remains of a tiny cabin clung like a limpet. This had been one of Harv's favourite "hides," from which he could spot deer many miles away along the shore or crossing on the ice. We climbed to Harv's lookout – to find that new people had taken possession.

A garish red-and-yellow signboard told us this was now

PIKES PEAK[*]

and a small sign next to it warned

DONT PISS INTO THE WIND.

The remains of Harv's deliberately inconspicuous little shelter had been lavishly decorated with chrome-plated junk from wrecked cars. A sign nailed across the one window (now broken) read:

LIQUOR ONLY SERVED TO MINERS.

But the humourless pièce de résistance was a nearby boulder upon which was painted in glossy black letters:

BLARNEY STONE

under which someone had added with a marker pen:

KISS MY ASS.

During that first visit to Ananias, I spent most of my time in Cliff's company but one day he provided me with a ten-foot birchbark

---

[*] *The name had doubtless been conferred in remembrance of General Zebulon Montgomery Pike, commander of the U.S. force that, during the War of 1812, invaded Canada to sack and burn Toronto. Killed there by an explosion initiated by his own troops, General Pike is honoured and memorialized in the United States by a real mountain that triumphantly bears his name.*

canoe that had once been Harv's favourite, a blanket, a grub box, fishing tackle, and basic camping gear and sent me off to paddle up an obscure little creek whose headwaters lay in a vast area of bog and muskeg called Black Swamp.

"Black Swamp," Cliff explained, "was Harv's special bailiwick – where the biggest bears and the most deer hung out. You could live like a king in there if you knowed a thing or two. I reckon you might know enough to stay alive, Squib, and you might *learn* something if you keep your eyes peeled and your ears clean.

"Might be you'll hear old Jo belling back in there somewhere. Jo was the best of Harv's hounds. He went missing soon after Harv flew the coop.

"Tell you the kind of hound he was – one time he had a sore foot so Harv left him behind when he was going hunting and Jo got real huffy and went off on his own. Harv went up the lake to that little tilt we was at on the cliff. He had the field glasses he'd took from a dead Jerry at the Somme when he was over there in the First War. Looking around, he sees a rumpus on the far shore of the lake so he puts the glasses to it and sees a big buck jumping around on the beach. It had lopsided antlers, but what caught Harv's eye was Jo – right up onto that buck's back, looking like he was stuck to it.

"How he got up there nobody'll ever know – maybe the buck got itself mired and he jumped it – but it was desperate to get shed of him. Couldn't shake him off so it took to the water and struck out for the other side, which was near a mile away.

"Harv watched the whole business. Said by the time they got over to his side the buck was pretty well played out and the dog half-drowned. As the buck staggered up the bank, Jo slid off and just laid there on the beach like a sack of moose shit. Harv said he could-a taken a long shot at the deer but didn't 'cause the buck was standing right over the dog. Then it seemed like Jo and the deer kind of sniffed noses and both of them shook theirselves and away they went – the buck into the bush and Jo along the shore, heading south.

"Jo was already home when Harv got back, and none the worse though he was still favouring his sore paw.

"Harv seen that same buck three or four times afterwards but never took a shot at him. Said he figured Jo wouldn't have like it if he had."

Harv's old canoe, a delicate little wisp of a thing that slipped through the water as easily as a loon, ghosted along so silently a muskrat snoozing on the bank failed to waken until I was so close it literally fell into the water in surprise. As I ascended the tea-coloured stream, I saw and heard many of its denizens going about their businesses. All of them, with the exception of the dozing muskrat, seemed unperturbed by my intrusion. On one stretch of quiet water, a sleek black otter accompanied me so closely I could have touched him with my paddle. When he eventually submerged, he did so without a ripple, leaving me feeling both elevated and humbled, as I might have been by a meeting with some primordial water spirit.

When the stream curved around the shoulder of a still-forested ridge, I went ashore and climbed it, hopeful of a view ahead and of perhaps hearing the distant belling of a spirit hound. Instead, I met a ghostlike marten who flickered at me disdainfully for an instant before vanishing up the bole of a towering white pine, which, with a few score of its fellows, had somehow escaped the timber butchers.

I camped that night on a sand spit just where the stream entered a balsam swamp. I made a small fire, filled my belly with brook trout caught ten minutes earlier, spread my blanket beneath the overturned canoe, and drifted off in a blue haze of wood smoke, balsam perfume, and the night music of frogs, an owl, and running water.

The first thing Cliff wanted to know when I returned to Ananias was whether I had come across any trace of Jo.

"Awful queer the way that dog disappeared. Was too damned smart to get hisself lost. Come from a line of dogs could find their way around better than birds.

"One time Jo's granddaddy – the first Jo – *did* go missing up around Gin Lake. Couple of months went by and still no sign of him so we figured he must be dead and gone. Then one October two years later a float plane landed on West Reach and taxied right in to our dock.

"When the door opened the first damn thing out was a dog. Come out like shot from a gun and jumped all over Harv 'til the old man pretty near fell off the dock.

"Two fellows got out and told us their story. Said they was lawyers from Kingston going north on a moose hunt. Said that two years previous they'd been hunting moose up near Gin Lake and come on a wolf snare with a dog caught into it by its hind leg . . . what was *left* of a dog, because it was nigh starved to death.

"Their guide was fixing to put it out of its misery but they liked the look of it and the long and short of it was they took it back to Kingston with them and got it fixed up good as new. And they was real happy when it turned out to be the best hunting hound they'd ever laid eyes on.

"The fall I'm talking about they'd rented a plane to fly them to Kaminiskeg Lake after deer, and they'd brought that dog along. The plane was flying high up crossing our lake when all of a sudden the dog like to took a fit, howling and yelling and jumping around 'til they feared he'd wreck the plane. Couldn't do nothing with him, so the pilot took the plane down and landed her.

"They was so mad they was just going to dump the dog and take right off again, but when they saw him and Harv crawling all over each other, they slowed up, and when we told them this was old Jo come home, they changed their minds. Couldn't believe he could be so smart!

136

"Didn't want to leave him then. But when they tried to get him back into the plane, Harv offered to go get his gun.

"'You fellows try to fly away with my dog and you're going to fly straight to hell,' he tells them.

"They left without Jo but on good terms with Harv, and next fall both come back and stayed at Ananias, and Jo and Harv took them hunting, and they got two prime bucks."

Although Harv did not hunt for "sport" (as the euphemism goes), he could and would kill any wild thing if its death contributed materially to the essential well-being of him and his family. On the other hand, should he encounter a wounded or crippled wild creature, even of a desired kind, he would sometimes bring it home alive and one of the children would be appointed its guardian. If it recovered, it would be returned to its own world.

"Harv was specially soft on beavers," Cliff recalled. "One winter he come on a young beaver with its front feet froze into a poacher's trap. He brought it back to Ananias, and the girls nursed it back to health even though both front feet rotted off.

"When spring come Harv turned it loose, but damned if it would go away. So he made a kind of lodge for it under the dock. It swum right into it and lived there four or five years and got along good enough to get itself a mate and a brood of kits every year.

"Many's the time I'd be out there fishing and old Two Foot or one of his bunch from under the dock would come alongside as if just to pass the time of day. They never slapped their tails. It was like they knew damn well that'd scare the fish away."

One day Cliff took me to visit the beaver dam at the mouth of Coburn Creek, which runs into the head of West Reach. It was a colossal structure at least a hundred and fifty feet long and up to ten feet high on the downstream side. The pond behind it was backed by a grassy muskeg containing one of the finest moose pastures in the country.

Cliff told me how one spring a mighty storm caused such a heavy runoff that the dam overflowed and threatened to collapse. For two days and nights the owners beavered to save it – then along came another heavy downpour.

"One way or t'other most of us hereabouts had a stake in that dam," Cliff explained. "Deer, bear, foxes, wolves, and plenty others used it for a bridge. Without it they'd have had to swim West Reach or plough through swamp for miles and miles. Our folk used it from the time they first come. It was wide enough to carry a wagon, and when I was a younker there was still a cart track across it. The moose needed the dam too because, though we et a good few of them, a good many more would have starved in hard winters without the swamp pasture beyond the dam."

Harv, who had been keeping an anxious eye on the threatened dam, concluded the beavers could no longer deal with the problem unassisted so he rowed back to Ananias and rousted out the entire human population – four grown men, half a dozen youths and children, and as many girls and women – armed them with axes, crosscut saws, and spades, and led them in skiffs and canoes to the aid of the beleaguered beaver.

Some cut trees into logs and rolled or carried these to the pond. Others used their canoes to tow logs or bundles of brushwood to the inner side of the dam, where they could be manoeuvred into place by women and children who also dug and hauled bucket after bucket of clay and mud with which to cement the additions into place.

As Cliff told it, "First off the beavers kept their distance but pretty soon they come back onto the job. Beavers and us worked together. When a girl dumped her pail of mud into a hole, pretty soon there'd be a beaver patting it down. Once, when Harv was trying to drive a pole into the front of the dam, a snaggle-toothed old beaver big as a dog come along and tried to steal it away. Was a sight to see, with Harv and that beaver tugging at that billet. Harv lost his temper.

"'Goddamn it!' he yelled. 'Let go or I'll kick your good tooth out!'

"The beaver hung on and, when Harv slipped and lost his grip, the beaver hauled the billet into deep water and floated it about fifty feet along, with Harv stumbling and cursing along the top of the dam.

"Harv almost fell into a new break he hadn't even knowed was there, but the beaver knowed. And that was where he put the billet, and the long and the short of it was, the dam stayed put."

Deer and moose were staple foods for Harv's extended family, which at any given time could include up to half a dozen adults and as many as a dozen youngsters. Hunting was not a recreation for those people – it was a vital function that elicited an almost religious attitude echoing the ethos of the aboriginal ancestors of us all.

"If you shot something when Harv was around," Cliff told me, "you made good and sure you killed it quick and clean. If he seen you take a gut shot he'd belt *you*, like as not. And if you just wounded something you had to stay onto it 'til you killed it dead, suppose it took all day and half the night.

"More'n once I seen Harv *hold* his own fire when a deer out-smarted the dogs as was trailing it. 'That there deer earned a second chance,' he'd say. One time a cow moose the dogs was running mired herself up to her belly so bad in a muskeg Harv could have just knocked her on the head. 'Stead of which he spent an afternoon cutting and hauling poles and jamming them under her 'til she could get good enough footing to scramble clear and get away.

"He could take a knock good as he gave. One time when my brother George was ten and I was twelve, he took us deer hunting and we come upon a gang of foolhens – spruce grouse, you call them – sitting all in a row on a branch like a bunch of old biddies at a Bible meeting, clucking and clicking away at us like we was the devil's spawn.

"Now Harv had told us kids time and again, 'Don't you kill fool-hens. Someday you might be caught out with no grub and no gun to get none, and ready to starve to death. Then a foolhen shows up and all you got to do is tap her on the head or wring her neck and there's your dinner. So leave them be unless you needs one bad.'

"He'd drilled that into us real good, but that day he was in a foul mood. We'd been out since dawn and got nothing, and the only chance he'd had for a shot at a deer his old gun misfired, which made him wild. Anyhow, when we come upon that bunch of foolhens Harv grabbed a little .22 off George and quick as a wink shot the head off one of the birds.

"George just stood there a second or two looking at his grand-daddy. Never said a word, but all of a sudden he cocked his arm and swung a punch right up from the ground to Harv's jaw.

"It knocked the old man's glasses up onto his forehead and sent his cap flying after the rest of the foolhens as George yells, 'Leave 'em be, you old bastid! Don't you know *nothin'*?'

"Harv was pleased as punch. Week or two later he proudly told our dad George had loosened two of his teeth and 'they ain't set yet!'"

The weather closed in on Ananias and Cliff and I found ourselves confined in Harv's house by pelting rain and furious gusts. We lit a big fire in the living room, did a little cooking, drank a modicum, and yarned a lot. Or, rather, Cliff yarned and I listened, occasionally egging him on.

"What about women?" I asked innocently. "Was Harv much interested in them?"

Cliff snorted – literally.

"Nope. Not so's you'd notice. Not more'n eight days of the week – not to mention the nights. Mind you, he *might* tickle any one of them come within reach and no doubt he *did* father his share of wood colts. Truth to tell, there wasn't many ladies round about he hadn't jumped, or tried to, one time or another. . . .

"'Cept for Leathy Grant.

"Leathy was Watt Grant's daughter, come to live with Harv and

Liza, his second wife, after Watt got drowned on a log drive down the Ottawa.

"Now Leathy was a good deal worse than just *shy* of men – she was plain man-scared. Would scream if one as much as looked her over. Was so goddamn flighty she wouldn't undress at night 'less every lamp in the house was out, fearful somebody might see her dimple.

"One time after Harv was getting a little long in the tooth, he was out digging potatoes and grunting and groaning every time he leaned over to pick one up 'cause of a bad back. I happened by, and asked him why he didn't get Leathy to do it for him.

"'*Leathy!*' he spits. 'Goddamn it, boy, *she* wouldn't stoop down in front of no potato! Potatoes got eyes, *ain't* they? Could peek right up under her skirt!'

"Harv wasn't much for religion so he steered clear of churches, though he never missed the revival meeting the Free Methodists held at the north end every August month.

"It lasted a week, under canvas. A real old-fashioned come-all-ye. Harv took me and George up there once when we was about half growed. Told us the revival was the best Christly jumping ground short of Heaven herself. And the proof was in the pudding – more babies was born in April month in our neck of the woods than all the rest of the year.

"All three of us was pretty well played out by the time we headed home. The kicker give out, and George and me had to row most of the way while Harv snoozed in the stern seat, with his 'leetle eye' opening every now and again just in case something come along.

"But let me tell you about Harv and Miss Adelaide.

"We never knowed where Miss Adelaide come from or who her folks was. What we heard, she was the oldest of three sisters come into the country from eastward before 1900 in a canoe paddled by an old fellow who might have been their daddy.

"When they smashed the canoe in a rapid on the Madawaska and lost pretty much everything they had, the old fellow put Miss Adelaide in charge of the others – told them all to stay put and he set off to see could he find help. And never come back.

"Miss Adelaide built a lean-to shelter then set the younger ones to looking for grub. They caught trout and suckers with their hands in a creek. Caught rabbits with snares made from willow roots. Picked berries in the bogs. But it was slim pickings, and when the old fellow never come back, one day Miss Adelaide gets the other two onto their feet and they pack up what little they had and set off on their own.

"Took a while, no doubt, but they made their way through swamps, around lakes, over brooks, and through the woods 'til they come upon the camp of an Algonquin family, and them people took them in.

"Now to git back to Harv – one time when he was still a young buck he'd been trailing a moose in Black Swamp for a couple days and was pretty well tuckered out when he come across a cabin in the middle of the swamp as had a sign nailed over the door that said:

MINK STATION

"Well, he didn't know what to make of that but he thumped on the door and a pretty woman about his own age opened it and said she was sorry but the track hadn't been laid so there wasn't no trains running yet. Said she was Miss Adelaide, the station agent, and did he want to come in and wait, though it'd likely be a while?

"Harv was flummoxed. Didn't know if she was right in the head or what. He knew there weren't no railroad into Black Swamp nor likely never would be. He couldn't figure out how this woman got there nor what she might be up to. What he *did* know was she was a good-looker and friendly as a puppy.

"He said she was built as neat as a young doe. Wore men's

knee-high lace-up boots, a fringed deerskin jacket, a short skirt, and a headband with beads all the colours of a rainbow.

"'She looked like an angel,' he said, but was able as a man. She had built herself that cabin; cut her own winter wood; drove dogs and run a trapline; and paddled her own canoe out of Black Swamp to visit and to get stuff from the Indians was still living on the land – maybe the same ones she'd happened on when she was just a kid.

"The way Harv told it, she could do pretty near anything he could. But she *did* seem a mite lonely. So he took up her invite . . . and it turned out to be good for all time.

"They never got married because both was as stiff-necked as cranes with rheumatics and Miss Adelaide claimed she was honour bound not to leave Mink Station 'til the railroad sent someone to relieve her. As for Harv, he wouldn't make an honest woman out of her 'til she was willing to move to Ananias, and she wouldn't budge.

"How did she get away into Black Swamp like that? Well, according to Harv, when she was about fifteen some white men camped near the Indian camp where she and her sisters was living. Said they were surveying for a railroad company was going to build a line through the swamp to get at the last big stand of virgin timber left in the country.

"They was led by a red-headed fellow who was more interested in Miss Adelaide than in surveying. He got what he wanted by telling her the company was going to build a station right in the middle of Black Swamp called Mink Station and he'd be in charge of it, and then he'd marry her and they'd be the king and queen thereabouts.

"When the redhead and his crowd went out that autumn, he promised to be back come spring. That winter she built the cabin where Mink Station was supposed to be. But, of course, he never did come back.

"She stayed on there by herself and wouldn't budge. Even after Harv found her, she still wouldn't leave, though he was welcome to stay at her place and in her bed long as he pleased.

"That being the way it was, Harv married a woman from Gilmour and got three young ones on her, one of them being my mother. But Mother died young so Harv took in Liza MacRae, a widow woman, and her sons. But he never did cut loose from Miss Adelaide – nor she from him.

"Early on Harv had give her a heavy old army whistle had a screech to it you could hear three, four miles off on a still night. When Miss Adelaide got to feeling lonely, she'd push off in her canoe if it was summertime, on snowshoes in wintertime, and travel from Mink Station to the big ridge behind Ananias. Then she'd lay into that whistle!

"When Harv heard it, he'd light out running. Liza couldn't abide Miss Adelaide nor nothing about her. So of an evening if things was a mite dull in Harv's house, one of us youngsters might straighten up in his chair and ask, 'You hear something? . . . Thought I heard a whistle. . . .'

"Liza would grab an iron skillet off the stove and just *dare* Harv to so much as stir from his chair. Generally he was too quick for her and he'd whip outside with her yowling after him. Which didn't do no good for he'd be gone.

"If it was a false alarm he'd come back madder than hell. But if it was the real thing, we might not see him again for quite a while. He had a little tilt somewhere up behind the ridge and that's where they'd be at it. When he *did* come home, looking that pleased and satisfied, Liza wouldn't speak to him for a week.

"One winter when Harv was off north timber cruising for the Gilmour Lumber Company, Liza laid one too many chores onto me and I decided to get even. The night we had the first snow of the season I put on a worn-out pair of woman's boots was in the back shed and slipped out and made tracks all around the place. Then I cached the boots and slipped back into the house and nobody the wiser.

"George was the first one outside next morning, fetching a load of firewood. He come back in so het up he was like to piss himself.

So Liza went out and had a look and all hell broke loose. She grabbed a hatchet and took off, yelling, 'I'll chop you up so fine, you black bitch, the ants won't find enough of you for breakfast!'

"Liza *stayed* on the boil 'til Harv come home. I figured she'd chew his head off, but she just hauled him into bed and jumped him so frequent I guess he was glad to go off for another round of timber cruising.

"It's a funny thing. Although I never laid eyes on Miss Adelaide myself, she seemed almost as close as my own kin. But after Harv went away for good, she was gone too – or almost gone.

"The winter after he packed it in, I happened to be here on my lonesome and got snowed in by a big blizzard. When the wind dropped out, the snow was piled up higher than my arse. It was still as death everywhere outside. There was no birds, not even a whiskey jack or a raven. Nothing flying. Nothing moving. But *some*body'd been out there. On racquets. And whoever it was had left a trail down from the ridge and right around the house.

"Must've been somebody pretty small, and light on their feet because the tracks weren't deep. And they was toed-in, Indian style. Whoever it was, they'd been followed by a dog walking in the racquet tracks like an old dog will.

"And no, Squib – afore you ask – I never heard no whistle blow. Not then. Nor ever after."

In the summer of the year Cliff turned fourteen, a swarm of prospectors descended on the country. Their camps sprang up like toadstools after a rain. The reek of their campfires was everywhere, and human and non-human residents alike were forced to flee forest fires deliberately set to expose the naked rock beneath.

The outlanders drifted secretively through gullies, up and down streams, and along the lakeshores, generally avoiding human contact, although occasionally one would show up at McAllister's store in

Gilmour. My regimental buddy Lorne McAllister was a teenager then and recalled them with contempt.

"They was dirty buggers, Squib. Dirty spoken and mean too. Would only buy a bit of flour, sowbelly, or tea, and they pinched every penny. We had little enough truck with them, nor they with us."

Wes'makoon people were not themselves interested in whatever gold might lie beneath their feet. Gold had never filled their bellies or brought them joy in the past. At best, outsiders who came sniffing after it were viewed with suspicion.

Suspicion became hostility when the intruders slaughtered pregnant does; pilfered from trapline caches (a cardinal sin amongst forest folk); failed to properly douse their camp fires; deliberately set wildfires; and scarred the land with "test holes" blasted into the bedrock.

Harv kept an especially close eye on them, as did Cliff, who viewed them with a boy's innate curiosity sharpened by suspicion.

On occasion Cliff would conceal himself overlooking the mouth of West Reach, his .22 crooked in his elbow, imagining he was an Algonquin brave and the stranger making his way unobtrusively down the lake in a nondescript canoe was the advance scout of an Iroquois raiding party.

Then Cliff would lay the foresight of his rifle on the unsuspecting prospector – and hold on him until he passed from sight behind a point of land.

Returning to Ananias, Cliff would tell his grandfather what he had seen.

"Bush devils!" Harv would grunt angrily. "Carrying on like they owns the world. Poaching the deer! Firing half the country! Bastids would steal gold outen your back teeth.

"Goddamn them all to hell. I knows them. Back before the big war I was up in Negeek Lake timber cruising when they come busting into that country. They was the devil's curse! Blazing claim lines all across the best deer runs, building corduroy roads across the best moose marshes, cutting or burning the best timber stands and staking every goddamn gold-showing even was it no bigger than a piss pot! I tell you, boy, they made a goddamn mess.

"They *did* find one good patch of pay dirt though and then some hog's ass from Toronto or New York or some such rat hole dug a mine and built a concentrator mill and hired every man and boy round about they could lay hands on to go underground like a bunch of goddamn moles.

"That was hard times so a good many men as should've knowed better went down that mine – and caught the gold fever themselves.

"They worked their asses off down there in the dark . . . until the gold give out. Then everything closed down. But the fellows who worked the mine and the mill never got themselves turned back around. So most of them left the country and went out front to scratch for wages. Their women folk helped drive them to it. They'd got used to having cash money in the hand.

"But men or women, they was gulled – the lot of them. Gulled by gold!"

"Granddad," Cliff asked the old man one day, "what *we* going to do about them fellers if they come looking for gold around our place?"

As Cliff recalled it, Harv had been standing at the head of the long kitchen table. He crouched down, spread his great hands wide, then clenched them as if around someone's throat.

"By the Lord livin' Jesus!" he roared. "Ary one of they shows hisself on West Reach I'll cuff him up to a peak and knock the christer's top right off!"

That triggered Liza.

"You blaspheming old fool! If the Lord don't strike you dead for carrying on that way, maybe one of them prospectors *will*. And it'll be no more than you deserve!"

Harv was not religious, but Liza surely was. At first light each Sunday she would begin loudly praying and continue at it until bedtime, interjecting hymn singing, shouted hallelujahs, and Bible readings. For his part, Harv made a practice of quitting the house before dawn on Sundays, nominally to go hunting.

Early one Sunday in June, he rousted Cliff out of bed to go hunting from a hide near a remarkable granite cliff called Elephant's Arse. It bore that name because it was huge, well-rounded in the right places, and vertically scored down the middle by a deep crevasse, up which a boy could shinny to the top before diving into the crystalline waters below. Generations of naked boys had plunged from Elephant's Arse – and countless deer had made use of the narrows just beyond it as a convenient place to swim the Reach.

On this particular Sunday, as Cliff remembered, "we toted a grub-box with a bottle of Harv's white lightning down to the dock and put it into the canoe. Harv took along his old .44.40 and let me have his .30.30. We got to the hide just before dawn. It was just a few poles covered with spruce boughs and a pile of dry bracken inside to lay on. I crawled in and went to sleep until maybe an hour later Harv poked me in the ribs.

"'Wake up, boy!' he says quiet like. 'They's something swimming past Elephant's Arse. . . . Could be a deer, maybe a bear. . . .'

"It was kinda misty and Harv's sight wasn't the best anymore. What *I* saw was somebody in a canoe ghosting along into the shadow of Elephant's Arse so close he looked to be part of it. When I said what *I* seen, Harv took another good hard look, then slammed his .44.40 to his shoulder.

"'Goddamn it to *hell*, boy, that ain't a *man* . . . it's a Christly *prospector!*'

"With that he thumbs back the hammer on the old gun, draws a bead, and yells at the top of his lungs, 'GET OUTTA HERE, YOU HELLHOUND!'

"Well, you know a .44.40 goes off like a cannon. The echoes when he took the shot sounded like a regiment of artillery letting loose. I never did know for sure what he aimed at – *if* he aimed at all – but I heard the whack of lead hitting *something* solid.

"I was scared to look. Maybe Harv was too. The quiet after the echoes faded was awful, but neither of us said a word. We was ready to slip out the back of the hide and head for home when we heard something queer – sounded like one of them big red-topped wood-peckers banging on a stovepipe, only it was coming from Elephant's Arse. We looked then, and we seen the feller hadn't *been* hit. Nor he hadn't made tracks out of there neither. He'd run the bow of the canoe into the crack and was standing up, banging away with one of those little prospector's hammers.

"Harv seemed kind of stunned as we hightailed it home, shaking his head and saying, 'What can you *do* with the kinda feller's got to be dead afore he's scared?'

"When we got back to the house, Liza went for us.

"'I heard that shot!' she yells. 'God in his Heaven musta heard it! Wonder he didn't strike the both of you down, banging away on the Sabbath like you was the devil come calling.'

"Harv never said a word – just took himself off and we never seen him again 'til next day.

"I tried to tell Liza what happened but that only made her flap her apron and hiss like a goose. After a time she calmed down a little and ordered me to paddle back to Elephant's Arse and fetch the pros-pector back for dinner.

"'Least you black heathens can do for that poor man! Now git!' was what she said.

"So I went back. The fellow was still working away from his canoe – a little squirt of a man hadn't shaved in a year or two. He paid me no heed at first and I had to ask him three times to come to our place for dinner before he stopped hammering. Finally he turns to me with a smile big as a sunset and says, 'Supposes as I might. Seems like fortune is blessing me this day.'

"Liza treated him like he was a long-lost brother. Nothing was good enough for him. She had made a big venison pie for Sunday dinner, but there was precious little of it left for me, and none at all for Harv when he did come home.

"The little feller never said much 'til he was full as a tick, then he pushed back from the table and says, 'A dee-licious *re*-past, the likes of which I haven't ate for many a year. My thanks to you, Ma'am. And to you, boy, if you was the one as fired. Your bullet struck a vein of quartz not two feet from me, and when I got the dust out of my eyes I sees a showing of gold I believe will assay thirty dollars to the ton. Good enough to put me on easy street the rest of my life. And now, if you'll excuse me, I got to hustle back there and stake my claim.'"

The months that followed may have been the worst in Harv Gunter's life. Word of the strike must have got around with lightning speed. If Harv stirred more than a few hundred yards from Ananias he was likely to encounter a claim post, for the country around was crawling with prospectors and Harv was convinced West Reach was doomed to become a mining camp. He hardly left the place all summer, and his rifle hardly ever left his side. Come fall a shortage of powder for reloading cartridges sent him to the store at Gilmour.

"As old man McAllister was weighing out the powder," Cliff told me, "he asked if Harv had seen anything of a bearded little prospector with a wild look about him. Harv started to tell him yes, then thought the better of it.

"'No, by the Lord livin' Jesus, I never seen that devil's spawn, nor ever wants to again! What about him?'

"Mac tells him the fellow had come into the store clucking like a hen partridge with a nest full of pipped eggs. Said he wanted to buy some grub but hadn't no money. Instead, he pulls out a baking powder can, unscrews the top, and spills a little pile of yellow flakes onto Mac's counter.

"'This here's better than money,' he says.

"Mac figured the poor bugger must have been born yesterday. Mac had worked in a gold mine in Quebec and knew what pyrite was, but he never called him on it. Give him a few dollars' worth of grub and the fellow went on his way, happy as a hound in spring.

"He never came back. Mac doubted he ever would. Figured the poor bastard most likely went right off his rocker when he found out what he had in his can was just fool's gold.

"When Harv got back to Ananias he told me about it then give me a hungry sort of a grin and says, 'Take a lesson from that, my boy. Don't never pull the trigger 'til you knows what's in your sights. I might of shot that son of a bitch stone dead and him as harmless as a burnt porcupine.'"

# · 6 ·

## INTERLUDE

$M$y visits to Wes'makoon and the time I spent with its denizens both human and otherwise, past and present, were a great solace to me, but ever since our trip to Europe our ten acres, which had seemed such a sylvan sanctuary in a world still reeling from the insanities of war, had begun to feel more like a subtle trap, and I was experiencing a recurrence of my post-war compulsion to flee the madding crowd.

Early in the summer of 1953, I had proposed to Fran that we take a year's leave of absence from the Albion Hills and spend it with the remnants of the Idthen Eldeli – the Dene people who still lived a semi-nomadic life to the north of Brochet.

"Theirs is the other half of the *People of the Deer* story," I explained. "It needs to be told – and I'd like to do the telling."

Although I did not expect her to be enthusiastic, I was taken aback by the vehemence with which she rejected the idea.

"Look!" she cried. "You're thirty-two years old and *I'm* almost thirty. Way past the best time to start a family. We *have* to start one *now*, and I want us to do it here in Albion!"

Although pleased by the prospect of paternity, I could feel the concrete hardening around my feet. The prospect of new obligations sent me back to my typewriter while taking what comfort I could from the "birds and the bees" who were moving onto our property in variety and abundance. *They* seemed content to be here, which *almost* made me feel I should be too.

Our small patch of swamp, scrub, and worked-out hillsides seemed to have become an irresistible magnet for the Others. Our pond was a hive of activity – spring peepers had laid their eggs in it and it was swarming with froglets. As the summer drew on, innumerable kinds of water bugs, beetles, and flies emerged. These in turn attracted a young painted turtle, spotted salamanders, more species of frogs and toads, several ribbon snakes, and a water shrew; some of these were presumably awaiting the transformation of the tadpoles into bite-sized froglets. The pregnant pond was also periodically reconnoitred by a great blue heron, a kingfisher, and a spotted sandpiper. A resplendent pair of wood ducks visited briefly but took a rain check, and I did not see them again until two years later, when another pair took possession of the pond.

The pond was also visited for a drink, a bath, or reasons I could only guess at, by all sorts of other creatures. These included a groundhog; a vixen who was raising her family in a den dug into our hill; a mink who left only her footprints in the mud to mark her visits; and, incredibly, an osprey – the great fish hawk – who hovered casually over our pothole for a few minutes as if to see how things were developing before taking herself off to more productive waters.

The pond produced never-ending surprises. On a day when the temperature was well above ninety degrees and the heat became more than I could bear, I shucked off my shorts and jumped from the end of my little wharf to stand naked on the muddy bottom in water barely up to my thighs.

Though almost as warm as soup, it felt wonderful. I was in a state of blissful relaxation when something hit my penis so sharply it sent me scrambling out of the water. Feeling somewhat foolish, I went to the end of the wharf and peered into the brown water for a glimpse of my assailant. Unable to see much, I cautiously lowered my hand with forefinger extended. There was a sudden swirl and I glimpsed a silvery something delivering a head-on charge.

It had to be a fish, but there *were* no fish in my pond – or should not have been, since no stream fed it. I had, however, "inoculated" it with a few pails of water scooped from a swampy little lake on a neighbouring property in an attempt to introduce spores, eggs, and cysts, together with minute adult forms of pond life and thus speed up the evolution of a natural and balanced aquatic habitat. Evidently the inoculation had included something unexpected.

After again poking my finger below the surface, and again having it unceremoniously bumped aside, I got my butterfly net. This time, when the finger was bumped, I swooped up an aptly named bull-head minnow, only three inches long but furiously indignant at finding itself cupped in my hand. I let it go at once for I had guessed its secret. Having glued a mass of eggs to the underwater woodwork of the dock, it was now on guard against any intruder who might pose a threat. A week later, when the water had cleared a bit, I found its nest – a lemon-sized, translucent jellylike mass filled with little sacs, each of which contained an embryonic minnow.

Every day thereafter until the eggs hatched, I made my peace with the little fish by scattering a few tiny earthworms, which it accepted with alacrity though continuing to attack my intruding finger. I gave it no second chance to reject any other part of me. (I later learned from a professional ichthyologist that my bullhead was almost certainly a male since, in this species, it is the male who guards the eggs until they hatch. I like to think that perhaps he was a bit jealous.)

The pond also played a role in attracting a wide variety of non-aquatic birds and terrestrial animals to our property. These included a pair of yellow-bellied cuckoos, who successfully nested in a bush ten feet from the edge of the pond; a cedar waxwing, who fledged five offspring in a spruce tree overlooking it; and a pair of almost-invisible grasshopper sparrows behaving like winged mice as they scuttled about the edge of the pond.

More than thirty species of birds chose to nest with us that year, and most of our co-residents seemed happy to take advantage of our hospitality. There were fox snakes in the fireplace, skunks and chipmunks under the house, and a flying squirrel who raised a brood in our attic. Even our bed was investigated by rambling deer mice – sometimes while we were in it.

The summer of 1953 grew hellishly hot, resulting in an exodus of Torontonians to the relative coolth of the Albion Hills. During July and August, the township roads, woods, valleys, and sylvan nooks were overrun by human intruders who all too frequently were obstreperous and sometimes threatening, tending to treat the countryside and its inhabitants with casual contempt.

Some drove their cars right up to our door and parked there while they investigated our pond for fish (there *were* none except for the beleaguered bullhead) or with a view to picnicking or swimming.

Some bristled when asked to move along; some grew threatening. I tried dealing with the latter by displaying my old army carbine, until it dawned on me that another tactic might be more successful. I began a sign campaign, arranging them strategically about the property:

DO NOT STEP ON THE SNAKES

and

BEWARE OF POISON IVY

and

HORNET STINGS CAN BE FATAL

The one that had the most salutary effect, however, was this:

DANGER

RADIATION HAZARD

to Unprotected Personnel

by order
Keewatin Research Authority

In those Cold War days the mushroom clouds of Hiroshima and Nagasaki still loomed ominously, so this was potent stuff. Once the radiation signs were in place we had no more unwanted visitors. *And few wanted ones* since for a time nobody would come through our gate without being assured of safe passage. Some local residents even took to avoiding the 30th side road entirely, and the township's road grader and gravel trucks became even more invisible than usual. This was, however, a small price to pay for the absence of vacuum cleaner and Fuller Brush salesmen, the Raleigh Man with his van of patent medicines, and Jehovah's Witnesses.

But then, one sunny day in August, a shiny Buick bearing the insignia of the Department of Health edged cautiously up to our door and out stepped two men in suits carrying briefcases, followed by two more in white coveralls carrying Geiger counters. They advanced upon me with the gravitas of pallbearers. Halting a safe fifteen or twenty feet away, one of the suits solemnly intoned the reason for their presence.

"It has been brought to the attention of the department that radioactive emissions are believed to be emanating from your property. All radioactive substances must be authorized, licensed, and inspected by federal authorities. Produce the relevant documents. After which we will inspect the premises and installations."

As if for emphasis, one of the Geiger counters suddenly emitted a series of clicks, eerily reminiscent of the warning given by a rattlesnake about to strike.

I hastened to reply.

"Look, I'm sorry, but we've actually got no radioactive stuff here. Never have had."

"What about the signs?" the spokesman demanded sternly.

"Ah, yes. Well, as anyone reasonably conversant with the English language might conclude, they mean that if you walk around here naked on a sunny day you're likely to get a bad sunburn."

A heavy silence followed. Then:

"*Don't you get flip with us, Mister!* We'll investigate, and if you're hiding anything, you'll find yourself in very serious trouble!"

Where upon they headed off into our swamp, the scientists out front swinging their Geiger counters suspiciously from side to side.

When they returned an hour later, they trudged past our house without giving it or us a glance and climbed into their Buick without a word. However, as the driver spun the machine in a tight circle that left ruts in our bit of lawn, he shouted out his window:

"Stupid punk! You'll pay for this!"

But we heard nothing more of the matter, and as summer drew on I noted in my journal:

*We're having a mammoth berry crop. Have already picked and preserved gallons of wild raspberries, thimbleberries and tame strawberries. Can't keep up with the garden, even with Murray to help.* [Murray Biloki, a ward of the Catholic Children's Aid Society, lived on a nearby farm.] *New root cellar is going to be damn near full of potatoes, squash, onions, carrots, parsnips, cabbages, and Brussels sprouts, plus a couple of barrels of apples we've scrounged from abandoned orchards. We've already trucked about 30 pounds of shelled peas, cut-up green beans, and a dozen home-grown chickens to Orangeville to store in a rented freezer locker. And we've bottled God knows how many sealers of shelled peas, sliced beets, cucumber pickles, and jams and jellies. For sure we won't starve but I'm getting bloody well tired of being a field slave.*

By the end of September, I was ready to exchange servitude to the soil for the tyranny of the typewriter, and not before time. McClelland & Stewart and the book committee of the Hastings and Prince Edward Regimental Association were becoming impatient with my lack of progress. On our part, we were running out of ready cash, and my relations with my U.S. publisher and agent were becoming strained. Max Wilkinson sent me a somewhat plaintive if philosophical note about this.

*If you insist on refusing to listen to what your [U.S.] publishers tell you, you must expect a spanking, together with a reduction in your income. Dudley and Little, Brown know what their market is. You must give heed. I suppose you can commit hari-kari if you want but please give a thought to your unfortunate agent. Listen, won't you?*

I did not tell Max that I was, in fact, listening, but to an inner voice that was stubbornly insisting I close my ears to the siren song of fame and fortune south of the border. I wrote in my journal:

*I'm fed up to the teeth with the lackey line, that the way to make it big is to suck up to Uncle Sam. Seems like half the people I meet, especially in Toronto, tell me I should move to the U.S. of A., or at least go there in spirit. They claim New York, Hollywood, etc., will fill my pockets if only I become a Yankee turncoat. Well, screw that! This buck-toothed little beaver ain't a-going to play that tawdry game.*

Christmas (never my favourite season) came and went and by the turn of the year it seemed a new ice age was upon us. January and February of 1954 brought a succession of storms that snowed us under while the thermometer in my weather station plunged to Siberian depths. Albion Township's only snowplough was nowhere to be seen. It was rumoured to have skunked off to Florida. Lulu Belle and I became local heroes because, in a precaution dictated by Fran's pregnancy, I had bought a blade-type snowplough for the little vehicle, with which I was able to ferry pregnant women, an elderly man who had attempted suicide, a colic-stricken child, and sundry other unfortunates out to the highway.

Despite the weather, Fran and I and our unborn enjoyed this winter. The fireplace roared defiance at the blizzards. We ate like kings and queens for we were both competent cooks. We were healthy, and for almost the first time since we had been married Fran seemed at peace with herself. Indeed, she was in such excellent psychic condition that, early in the new year, when Angus wrote to ask if there was any chance I might be able to accompany him on a voyage to Halifax in *Scotch Bonnet* in June, Fran's response was entirely positive.

"Of course you must go," she said firmly. "Your father's only got one good arm and he's not young. Our baby will have been born by then and my parents are really anxious to come out and help for as long as we need them. Tell Angus yes."

Thus was the die cast – and neither Fran nor I had any inkling of the consequences.

# ‧ 7 ‧

## SAILING TO THE SEA

On the night of March 31, 1954, there came a very hard frost. The roads had become mud wallows and sinkholes from the spring melt. Since Fran's delivery date was almost upon us, I decided to make a run for it. Lulu rose to the challenge, and that night Fran lay in a hospital bed where, on April 4, Robert Alexander (Sandy) Mowat was born.

I was unable to bring Sandy and his mother home for two long weeks because spring rains made the 30th side road impassable to anything without wings or webbed feet.

Sandy was a hale and hearty child, and no more demanding than any other but his arrival on the scene made me take my responsibilities more seriously. As soon as the earth was fit to till I began, with Murray's help, to enlarge the vegetable garden again, expand the orchard, plant a raspberry and an asparagus patch, and set out three thousand more wildwood saplings.

One day while we were planting the trees I casually asked Murray if he would like to come along on a voyage down the St. Lawrence River to the Atlantic Ocean.

"My father will be the captain – it's his boat," I explained. "And I'll be the mate. You'd be the dogsbody – kind of a cabin boy and general factotum, if you know what that is. If you don't, well, you'll find out . . . but wait a minute . . . can you swim?"

Murray shook his head.

"Damn. . . . Well, you can learn. We won't be leaving for a few weeks so I'll teach you in the pond."

Murray was so confounded by the whole proposal that he hurried off to the Finnerty farm (which had been his home and his world for the last fourteen of his sixteen years) looking as stunned as if kicked in the head by one of the Finnerty heifers. But at six o'clock next morning when I opened the door to let the dog out, he was there.

"Mr. Farley," he said, "*I'm coming!* See, here's me bathing suit! Aunt Jane made it up for me last night and gave me a new rosary to go with it. But she says I *got* to learn to swim or I can't go."

Learn he did, in a froggish sort of a way. Since the pond was only four feet deep, the temptation to put his feet on bottom was more than he could resist. However, when I certified to Jane Finnerty that he could stay afloat (no matter how briefly) she reluctantly allowed her ward to embark on his first sortie into the big world beyond the Albion Hills.

On June 1 Fran's parents arrived from Toronto, their car loaded with baby gear, food, and presents for their new grandchild. They had reproachful looks for me. Perhaps they felt I was frivolously abandoning my parental duties. Nevertheless, they assured me things would be well looked after during my absence.

Three days later, Fran drove Murray and me to Malton Airport to board a twin-engined plane for his first flight – a noisy, bumpy one to Montreal where Angus and *Scotch Bonnet* awaited us.

———

*Scotch Bonnet* was the realization of my father's enduring dream. Having been an avid sailor since childhood on Ontario's Bay of Quinte, he had ever since kept an eye peeled for the ideal vessel in which someday to sail the deep and briny ocean. In 1937, just after he turned forty-two, he found his Dream Ship lying at a mooring in Montreal. A Norwegian double-ender, she was thirty-six feet long, ketch-rigged, and fitted with an auxiliary engine. Called a *redning-skoite* in her native country, she had been designed and built to serve as a pilot boat on the North Sea, one of the world's most demanding and unpredictable bodies of water.

Neglected, with peeling paint and an abandoned air, she was not very prepossessing – but she *was* for sale. My father fell instantly in love. He later wrote:

"She was my Dark Lady . . . down at heel, lonely, but so beautiful. In my mind's eye I could see her resurrected, garbed in glistening ebony with a golden waterline, her red sails straining as she and I drove through a foaming gap in the coral ring surrounding some South Sea atoll. . . . There was never a moment's hesitation. I *had* to have her come hell or high water! I didn't tell your mother, Farley. And I didn't tell you either. I just went ahead and bought her . . . *freed* her from servitude . . . and that was that."

He named her after a naked rock jutting out of Lake Ontario some miles off Presqu'ile Point. Although now inhabited only by gulls and cormorants, Scotch Bonnet Island was home in my father's youth to a light-keeper's family who had a girl of Angus's own age. When the weather was propitious, Angus sometimes sailed his little catboat out to the rock to visit her. Had she not died of typhus shortly before the onset of the First Great War, he might well have married her.

Memories of my own first summer aboard *Scotch Bonnet* (I was just Murray's age at the time) are full of happy sounds, images, and smells: the reassuring rattle of the anchor chain paying out at a mooring in Prinyer's Cove; the rich smell of glutinous mud on the "hook" when the anchor was hoisted aboard again; the snap and crackle of *Bonnet's* heavy canvas as she reached before strong winds off Point Peter; spray whipping across my face as a stiff gust laid her over on her side. But most of all I feel the vibrancy of her passage through wind and water while I brace myself at her helm, both arms straining to keep the oak tiller steady so the little ship will hold her destined course.

*Scotch Bonnet* became a part of me during the short time before the war began in 1939. When I went overseas to "do or die," Angus used her to bolster my spirits. As the dreadful massacre mounted to a crescendo, he promised she would be mine to sail anywhere I might choose – when I returned home again. He was throwing me a lifeline, and I seized it. The little ship became my talisman.

However, once the war was over and I was safely back in Canada, Angus said nothing more about her becoming mine. He never again raised the subject and I, in my pride, let the matter lie. When he invited me to join him on a voyage to Halifax where he was to give a speech at a national library conference, I thought he might be trying to make amends. It did not matter. The truth was I could not possibly have rejected such an invitation.

Murray caught his first sight of *Scotch Bonnet* as she lay at anchor in the basin of the Royal Montreal Yacht Club, her ebony-black hull contrasting sharply with the gleaming white yachts anchored all around her. Heavily built and broad of beam, she seemed as out of place as a water buffalo amongst a herd of gazelles, but I thought she looked as ready for whatever might come as one of Admiral Horatio Nelson's Hearts of Oak. Murray did not share my confidence.

"Jeez!" he pleaded after staring at her for a long minute. "Are we supposed to go out on the ocean in *that*?"

"Buck up. *That* will take you to hell and gone. And get a move on, will you? The captain's rowing the dinghy in to pick us up."

Obediently Murray followed me out on the club dock, but muttering to himself, "To *hell* and gone? To hell and *gone*? . . ."

"Welcome aboard, both of you," my father said briskly as he brought the dinghy alongside *Scotch Bonnet* and we clambered up on her deck. "And you, my lad," he added for Murray's benefit, "wipe the manure off your boots and put on this bonnet. It's a *scotch* bonnet, ye ken? You'll wear it whenever you're on deck, to show the world you belong to a seagoing vessel, not some rich stockbroker's toy. Come below now and we'll have a drink on it."

Sitting at the cabin table, Angus and I polished off a noggin and discussed his plans while Murray tentatively, like a cat in a new house, explored the little ship that would be our home for nearly a month.

She was well prepared. A huge war-surplus Carley Life Float of the kind carried aboard merchant ships during the war was lashed to the topside of the cabin. And about a dozen cork life preservers were inside, some serving as cushions on the cabin benches, others as pillows in *Bonnet*'s four bunks or cluttering up the tiny head. They were a damned nuisance, but they did seem to give Murray confidence. Food, including canned beef and hardtack biscuits of Nelson's era, was everywhere: under the benches, in the clothes lockers, in the bilges, above and below the bunks; and a bag of potatoes was sprouting in the Carley Float.

By 8:00 a.m. next day, we were in the entrance lock of the St. Lawrence Seaway on our way to the Atlantic Ocean. The gods were kind – allowing us to pass without incident through a formidable concrete canyon able to contain a twenty-thousand-ton ship. But the second lock became a fearsome ordeal when *Bonnet* found herself behind two large freighters. The great lock doors closed, and we were swirled about in an enormous box with two huge ships, either of which could have crushed our little vessel against the walls as easily as a man might crush a cockroach.

Escaping with pounding hearts, we skittered under innumerable bridges into the industrial heart of Montreal where the locks began again. Their walls towered far above *Bonnet's* mastheads as Niagaras of whitewater poured down upon us through holes in the massive walls, and the huge, half-submerged propellers of freighters turned within yards of our bowsprit.

We sidled and crept through six terrifying locks in all. Murray acquitted himself well despite having to deal with frantic and often conflicting orders issued in the strange argot of the sea. But as we were spat out of the final lock, he grimaced and muttered, "Ain't *never* going on no boat again when I get out of this one! Them jeezly locks scare the shit clear out of me!"

By the time we were released, we had been in the toils of the canal for seven hours.

Free at last, we "steamed" at full throttle – a deceptive term in the *Bonnet* equalling about six knots. This took us past the eastern out-skirts of Montreal into the relative calm of the St. Lawrence River meandering between low, lush, and shallow banks. The ship channel contained a steady flow of big vessels upward or downward bound so we kept *Bonnet* as close as possible to the black buoys at the edge of the channel, not venturing out of it for fear we would run aground and be swamped by the wash from the big ships. Our tension was eased briefly by a flock of about a hundred of the small geese called brant nonchalantly swimming about in mid-channel, stuffing them-selves with crane flies and blissfully ignoring the mighty behemoths bearing down on them from east and west.

By early evening, we were abeam of the shipbuilding town of Sorrel and, exhausted, decided to spend the night there. We steered *Bonnet* into the town's small-boat basin, where a conspicuous sign on a hotdog stand ashore announced that this was the CLUB DE YACHT DE SORREL. The club's sole employee seemed surprised to see us, but filled our gas tank and sold us a nylon *fleur-de-lys*, which we hoisted to our forestay as required by nautical tradition.

Angus spread his sleeping bag on deck to dry. Earlier that afternoon, he had been snoozing in the forepeak when we were passed by a fast French freighter whose bow wave came boiling down through *Bonnet's* fore hatch, almost washing Angus and his bed into the scuppers.

Sorrel seemed to have a properly Gallic character, with outside staircases, abundant ornamental iron work, useful-looking little shops, and a lot of pretty girls. So Angus and Murray went sightseeing while I tried to find parts for our twenty-five-year-old engine. Although its externals had been cleaned and even polished regularly, its innards did not appear to have been touched or, perhaps, even looked at since the engine's birth. My immediate concern was that the generator would not charge the batteries and that one of the engine's four cylinders had gone on strike. But although Sorrel's shipyards could and did build icebreakers, giant tankers, naval vessels, and freighters, they were unable to produce the humble parts I needed.

*Bonnet* lay moored to the breakwater, and there, in the calm of a lovely summer evening, we had a drink or two to toast our first day on the Great River. According to our patent log (a brass cylinder that we towed behind *Bonnet* to record distance travelled through the water), we were now fifty-five miles closer to the sea. Since we still had some twelve hundred miles to go, this was a trifling accomplishment, but we celebrated anyway. After a dinner of canned spaghetti garnished with canned sardines, Angus got out his venerable banjo and we sat on deck serenading passing ships out on the river with seamen's shanties from the old days of sail.

We left Sorrel soon after dawn to thread the tortuous channel through Lac Saint-Pierre, a vast shallow basin stretching out of sight to the northeast. Clinging as close as we dared to the edge of the buoyed channel again, and still under power because there was no wind to fill our sails, we puttered along through flocks of brant fattening up on crane flies for the rest of *their* journey from South America to high arctic breeding grounds.

Then the engine – the bullgine, Angus always called it – failed, leaving *Bonnet* adrift. Angus and I frantically tried to make repairs while Murray, alone on deck, clutched the useless tiller and watched apprehensively as block-long grain carriers from the upper Great Lakes, and massive ocean freighters from as far away as Ceylon, bore implacably down upon us. We must have been a trial to the river pilots at the helms of those big vessels as they tried to avoid converting us into minced meat and our little vessel into kindling. We diagnosed the bullgine's problem as a plugged fuel line that we eventually cleared by blowing (sometimes sucking) the dirt out and got underway again.

Just beyond Lac Saint-Pierre we began seeing vessels more our own size. They were *goélettes*, roughly built schooners, family-owned and family-worked. They had a casual and friendly air that drew us to them. Some miles above Quebec we came upon several anchored in a cove and, with engine trouble again upon us, we sought sanctuary amongst them.

Their people told us they were waiting for the tide to rise before continuing upstream to deliver cargoes of pulpwood to a paper mill. We had not realized that the ocean's tides penetrated this deeply into the continent, for we were freshwater sailors who knew little about such arcane things. The *goélette* people explained that when tide and current were *both* flowing eastward, it was foolish to waste costly gasoline trying to buck them.

"*C'est bon pour vous*," they said. "You go *down* the river. We go *up* . . . but not until after supper, when the tide is change."

Several men came aboard to sip our rum and listen to our laments about the bullgine. Then they produced a fuel filter and a roll of copper tubing and installed a new fuel system for us, refusing to accept any payment. They even politely refused to share the dinner I had cooked.

I had made a sausage ragout served on a bed of steamed rice. But *Bonnet* had no refrigeration and the sausages had been aboard so long they had turned a purplish-green. Moreover, the carrots were mouldy and the onions soft and slimy. As a final touch, kerosene had somehow managed to permeate the rice. Delicious aromas wafted from the galleys of the *goélettes* as we three surreptitiously scraped most of our supper overboard. I *did* keep the pot of rice and next day tried to turn it into a "dessert" by adding dried figs, cocoa, canned milk, and a bit of marmalade. Neither Angus nor the usually insatiable Murray asked for a second helping.

With the tide speeding the river current eastward, we started the bullgine, and the *goélette* people waved us on our way. Darkness fell, and Murray and my father went below as my watch began. I took considerable satisfaction in being able to identify each navigation light as it winked into being across dark waters and in steering a straight course toward it. There was less pleasure in steering so confidently when I eventually realized I was following the masthead light of a big ship bound for God alone knew where. Nevertheless, we made a good passage that night, reaching Quebec an hour before dawn.

I was about to drop into my bunk when we were hailed by an approaching motor launch. The burly fellow who clambered from it was Captain Robert Naish, skipper of the *Foundation Josephine*, a large, seagoing rescue tug berthed a mile away. Naish told us he had come at the request of my aunt Frances Thomson, secretary to the president of a company called Foundation Maritime, who had asked him to brief us on the difficulties we might encounter on our passage to the sea. Captain Naish did this with great thoroughness, while inflating our egos by punctiliously addressing Angus as Captain Mowat, as if the two shared equal professional stature.

After refuelling we passed close under the grim walls of the mighty Citadel and came abreast of *Foundation Josephine* – a sleek and powerful vessel possessing something of the aura of a naval ship. I rather importantly saluted her with three toots from the tin trumpet that served as our foghorn and *Josephine* gallantly replied with three mighty blasts from her siren that resounded all around the harbour. I glanced involuntarily over my shoulder to see if some royal yacht warranted the commotion. But it was only us. We straightened our bonnets, grinned smugly at one another, and left Quebec astern.

We passed downriver with the old city sun-hazed behind us, the magnificence of Montmorency Falls to the north, and the gigantic hull of the world's largest tanker in a shipyard on the south shore. A storm threatened but we did not care for we were in an exuberant mood.

We thought our troubles were behind us. The bullgine thought otherwise. As we cleared the foot of Orleans Island, it began to sputter and balk, forcing us to spend the rest of the night mostly adrift while we drained its clogged pipes, each time praying there would be enough juice left in the batteries to start it one more time. The channel remained far too narrow for comfort and was crowded with hurrying ships, including a huge passenger liner to whom *Bonnet*, with her black hull and her tiny oil-lamp navigation lights, must have been almost invisible.

Nightfall was made worse by the onslaught of a summer storm that cut visibility to nothing, and the traffic grew heavier until it seemed to us that every damn ship in the North Atlantic had chosen this particular night to sashay up or down the river. Skittering back and forth, we would sometimes try to sneak in behind a down-bound vessel then churn along in her wake as long as we could.

At one point we became aware of a peculiar frothing in our own wake. A great light dawned on Angus, and he leapt below to the pump in the galley sink. He reappeared a moment later with a glass of water that he thrust toward me. I tasted it and sputtered, for it was salt water. Although we were still nearly a thousand miles from the sea, the tide had brought the sea to us.

Dawn found us off Goose Cape on course for Murray Bay, the nearest harbour where we thought we might be able to find help for our ailing engine. But we found little aid in Murray Bay, home to Manoir Richelieu, a vast hotel with a castle complex catering to rich tourists. Like the inhabitants of most tourist towns, the locals were querulous and grasping. They filled our fuel tank but offered no solutions to our other problems. Frustrated and grumpy we limped back into the river stream, where the bullgine died again. Luckily a breeze sprang up so we hoisted all sail and were soon belting downstream fast enough to nearly match the pace of the big ships.

Because of an enduring anachronism in the international Law of the Sea (applicable to *all* navigable waters, fresh or salt), which stated categorically that a vessel under sail had the right of way over one propelled by an engine, we now had an advantage over the big fellows. This was a heady prospect, though not one we were anxious to put to the test.

I spent much of this day in the "engine room" – a space under the cockpit almost wholly occupied by the engine, leaving just enough room for one man to wriggle about. With the overhead hatch in place, there was no daylight so a flashlight had to serve. After what seemed like endless hours of poking about, I discovered that a minute crack had developed in the exhaust manifold through which water – *salt* water now – was spurting to short-circuit the coil and sometimes the spark plugs too.

My cure for this was to construct a sort of baffle out of an empty soup can and fix it to the manifold with a length of wire. Then I crawled out of my dungeon and Angus, who was at the tiller, tentatively pressed the starter. The bullgine coughed, failed, and coughed again. Then all three good cylinders fired, and soon she was running as robustly and steadily as anyone could wish.

We were in the North Channel not far from the mouth of the Saguenay River when Murray, on lookout in the bow, spotted a large, corpse-white something just beneath the surface directly in our path. At his shout I hauled the tiller hard over and *Bonnet* swung to port. We avoided a collision but came close enough to recognize the almost-submerged object as a twenty-foot-long beluga whale, one of a population of these normally arctic sea mammals which had colonized the river's estuary eons earlier.

This beluga was clearly sick or injured for it made no move to avoid us and even seemed to have difficulty keeping the breathing hole on the top of its barrel-sized head above the surface. An exhalation of its breath stank so strongly of decay that Murray covered his mouth and nose with his hands.

As *Bonnet* drew away, a black-backed gull, as much a harbinger of death at sea as the vulture is on land, swooped past to alight upon a small exposed portion of the whale's back and begin ripping up skin and blubber with its long, hooked beak.

Murray was much distressed by his first encounter with one of the Great Ones of the Deeps. I assured him we would meet more belugas, probably many more, and told him how, in 1946 when I was returning to Canada aboard a Dutch freighter, I had stood on her bridge as we were passing the mouth of the Saguenay and seen half a dozen pods totalling perhaps fifty or sixty white whales sporting around our lumbering ship. I also told him of having seen several of the truly great whales – blues and fins – as well as sei and pilot whales in the waters we were now entering.

"Where the Saguenay empties into the St. Lawrence," I told him, "we cross the hundred-fathom line, which means we'll have six hundred feet of very cold water under our keel. That cold water welling up into the warm river water is full of nutrients producing an explosion of plankton that attracts pods of every sort of whale. So many used to gather here to feed that ships' crews were sometimes scared to sail after dark for fear of hitting whales and sinking their own vessels.

"Sometime before the year 1500 – before Columbus, anyhow – this whale bonanza was discovered by European fishermen, mostly Basques, who began coming here with dozens of big ships to harpoon whales for oil and for a kind of springy bone called baleen that the plankton-eating whales grow in their mouths as strainers.

"The Basques named the region Bay of Whales – well named, because it took the whaling fleets of Spain, Portugal, France, England, the U.S.A., and finally Norway nearly four hundred years to do it, but by 1939 they had butchered so many whales here that the whaling business itself was about to go belly-up.

"Then the war came along and gave the remaining whales a second chance because people were too busy killing each other to hunt them. Though some *were* still killed by floating mines, by warships and submarines blowing each other up, and by planes using whales for target practice, the whales did get a bit of a breather and their numbers began to climb again.

"When I came this way in 1946, the place was beginning to reclaim its old name and fame. If you keep your eyes skinned you should see a good few from here on."

I was dead wrong about that. The *only* whale *Bonnet* encountered during the whole of her long voyage to Halifax, south to New York, and eventually back to Lake Ontario was that one sick beluga we met near the Saguenay.

As evening fell the breeze freshened, filling *Bonnet's* red sails until they were "hard and by," and sending her bounding along almost fast enough to overtake a rusty old Greek freighter. Neither Angus nor I got much rest that night since it needed two of us to steer and to handle sail because there was a plague of steamers on the estuary.

However, since we now had plenty of water under foot, we took to ignoring the buoys and sailing more or less where the wind would take us – and where big ships dared not go.

We had now travelled so far north that dawn brightened the sky at 2:30 in the morning and a red sun oozed over the horizon an hour later as we bowled along past Father Point pilot station, where several big ships idled in the stream waiting to drop off or take on river pilots.

At breakfast time, we altered course for Rimouski harbour where, as Captain Naish had told us, another Foundation Company tug was stationed whose skipper would brief us about the waters of the Gulf, now a little less than two hundred miles ahead. After feeling our way past a wreck in the harbour mouth, we spotted a rather elderly looking tug bearing Foundation Company's white-and-green colours on her funnel. As we headed for her, a tousle-haired fellow, dressed more like a farmer than a deep-sea mariner, stepped out on the wing of the bridge and beckoned us alongside. A deckhand took our lines and made us fast while Captain Ira Powers told us he had received a radio call from Naish asking him to look out for "a little black sail-boat with three Scotsmen aboard."

Powers, a native Nova Scotian, invited us to join him for an enormous "bluenose" breakfast featuring pickled herring and cold fatback pork then took us into his chart room for a briefing about what lay ahead. He was concerned we might have trouble with a massive causeway being built across the Strait of Canso to link Cape Breton Island with mainland Nova Scotia. He warned us that if we hoped to go through the Gut, as he called it, we had better get a move on because the narrow gap still remaining in the causeway was about to be closed, and it would be months before a lock and canal through it was completed. If we missed this window, circum-navigating Cape Breton would add almost three hundred miles to our trip.

But, just a week earlier, he told us, *Vera* had been summoned to the aid of a big freighter that had been flung so violently against the rim rocks, while trying to get through the gap against a rising tide, that she had torn a ten-foot hole in her bow and had to be towed to Halifax for repairs.

Seventy-year-old Powers, who had been going to sea – mostly in tugboats – for half a century, liked to yarn. During the war he had towed many disabled merchant ships to safety in Nova Scotia, Newfoundland, east-coast United States, and Icelandic ports after they had been savaged by winter storms or, worse still, by the torpedoes, guns, and bombs of German U-boats and long-range planes.

I also spent several hours with the *Vera*'s first mate, who had soldiered in First Division in Italy. Over a drink of rum to celebrate our survival there, we recalled the hell of Cassino when twelve hundred of our biggest guns had opened fire on the Hitler Line fortifications blocking our advance, and wave after wave of RAF and U.S. bombers had dropped their lethal loads into the inferno below.

Surprisingly, the mate considered that *the* most horrific explosion he had ever experienced had occurred here in the St. Lawrence River. In November of 1950 he had been skippering a *goélette* out of the north-shore village of Saint-Siméon. His vessel was at anchor waiting for the tide to turn when "Hell blew up on the river south of Saint-Fidèle. Was so goddamn loud I could not hear good for a week. Smoke and water shot up so thick it was like night right across the river to Kamouraska."

"What the devil happened?"

He shrugged. "Nobody knows for sure. Later, the radio say a Yankee plane drop a bomb by mistake. When we sailed for Rimouski couple of hours after, dead fish was floating in the water so thick it look like winter ice going out. Dead seals and white whales floating around too. Lots of them. There was a big stink of rotten fish along the shore all the way to Gaspé for weeks after."

"You never found out what blew up?"

"Never! Some foolish people said it might be a Russian air raid. Some said might be an ammunition ship sunk during the war finally blew up, but nobody can say *what* ship that could have been."

*Scotch Bonnet* got underway early next day and the mysterious explosion slipped out of mind until many years later when, at a time that I was publicly denouncing the stationing of American nuclear weapons on Canadian soil, I recalled what *Vera's* mate had told me – and wondered. I did not pursue the matter then and almost half a century would have to pass before the true nature of the "incident" on the St. Lawrence River in 1950 would become clear to me.

In the summer of 1950 the U.S. government asked the Canadian government for permission to station a force of armed nuclear inter-continental bombers at the Canadian air force base in Goose Bay, Labrador, as a counter measure to a perceived threat of nuclear attacks on North America by the Soviet Union. Canada was assured that the deployment would be temporary, lasting no more than six weeks, and would be implemented with such secrecy that nobody – certainly not the Canadian public – would ever be the wiser. Early in August, Prime Minister Louis St. Laurent acceded to the request, despite public declarations by his government that Canada would never allow nuclear weapons to be stationed on its soil.

By August 30, the 43rd Bombardment Wing of the U.S. Strategic Air Command (SAC) had established itself at Goose Bay. The Wing was staffed by 616 officers (mainly air crew) and 3,560 other ranks, and equipped with 36 B-50A[*] intercontinental bombers capable of carrying enough atomic weapons to destroy a number of Soviet cities.

---

[*] *The B-50A was an updated version of the B-29, Superfortress workhorse heavy bomber of the USAF during the closing years of World War II.*

The operations diary of the 43rd's security section records: "Upon arrival at destination the bomb carriers were met and cleared by Air Police security [and the bombs] were unloaded from the bomb carriers and taken to a restricted storage area . . . in a forest approximately 4 miles from the base where they were stored 1500 feet from the nearest road. Each unit was guarded 24 hours a day."

Once operational at Goose Bay, 43rd Wing, like the fabled camel in the Bedouin's tent, showed no inclination of ever leaving. It was still flying out of Goose Bay when I visited that air base in 1953 and did not leave, in the end, until 1971.

During this occupation there was a continuous interchange of men and equipment between 43rd Wing and its permanent home at Davis-Monthan Air Force Base near Tucson, Arizona, and nuclear bombs were routinely flown back and forth between Labrador and Arizona for inspection and adjustment. On the morning of November 10, 1950, one was loaded aboard B-50 No. 46-038 of the 43rd's 64th Bomber Squadron. The aircraft was airborne shortly after noon with its eight-man crew and a monster in its belly.

This was a Mark IV version of Fat Man, the nuclear fission bomb that in 1945 had all but obliterated the Japanese city of Nagasaki. Its core was a sphere of plutonium (Pu-239) surrounded by a sphere of uranium (U-235) which weighed about 445 pounds. This in turn was embedded in the middle of another sphere, about four feet in diameter, consisting chiefly of 4,895 pounds of the high explosives RDX and TNT. At detonation, the chemical explosives were designed to produce an *implosion* which, sequentially (and almost instantaneously), would crush the inner spheres, initiating a nuclear reaction to produce an explosion equal in power to that of 21,000 tons of TNT.

This particular bomb had been made "safe for transit" by the removal of the plutonium sphere through a tube built into its core. (The plutonium was referred to as "the pit" because it was at the centre of "the fruit.") Temporarily separated from its Fat Man, the pit nevertheless travelled with it. The uranium remained in place within the bomb because it could not be removed without dismantling the entire weapon.

The pilots and navigator of bomber 46-038 began their flight on a course designed to take them west and south across the Canada–U.S. border somewhere in the vicinity of Sault Ste. Marie. After only a few hours, however, the plane ran into trouble when first one, then a second engine failed, leaving just two to keep the bomber airborne.

When desperate efforts to restart the stricken engines were unsuccessful, the crew knew they had either to abandon the bomber in flight or attempt an emergency landing. Bailing out was not really an option. The potential consequences when the unmanned plane inevitably crashed were too horrendous to contemplate. An emergency landing had to be attempted – *if* a suitably equipped airport could be reached.

While the captain and navigator urgently conferred, the bomber was labouring in the vicinity of the little north-woods settlement of Chibougamau, 250 miles to the northwest of Quebec City. The nearest airport equipped to handle a B-50 with nuclear material aboard was an SAC base at Van Buren, roughly 440 miles to the eastward, on the U.S. side of the border between Maine and New Brunswick. Van Buren it had to be. However, to have risked a landing there with two engines out and a Fat Man nuclear bomb aboard would have invited an explosion that could have obliterated Van Buren as well as the Canadian town of Saint-Léonard, just across the Saint John River. So Fat Man had to go.

Strategic Air Command standing orders stipulated that if an atomic bomb had to be jettisoned over friendly or neutral territory, the drop should be made into a large expanse of open water where the consequences could be expected to be less disastrous than over land. Only one suitable drop zone existed on the new course of the crippled Superfortress 46-038 – the St. Lawrence River between

Tadoussac and Murray Bay, a stretch of water some forty miles long and up to eighteen wide, with depths as great as six hundred feet.

Shortly before 1600 on November 10, 1950, the B-50's bomb bay doors swung open and the Fat Man was dropped.

Next day the *Montreal Gazette* reported that St-Alexandre-de-Kamouraska on the south shore of the St. Lawrence River had been rocked by a mighty explosion. The *Canadian Encyclopedia* records that townsfolk saw a thick cloud of yellow smoke spiralling up a thousand metres above the middle of the river. Then came a low rumble that shook houses for forty kilometres around.

*Vera's* mate had described to me a smoke or vapour pillar towering so high it mingled with the cloud deck overhead. He thought the explosion must have taken place ten or fifteen miles to the south of Saint-Siméon where his vessel was lying. A subsequent wave surge from that direction nearly caused his *goélette* to break out her anchor and go adrift.

Some time after the event, the U.S. Air Force issued a succinct notice to the effect that one of its four-engined bombers had accidentally dropped some 500-pound practice bombs into the St. Lawrence River while on a training flight.

There the matter rested until almost fifty years later when the Canadian Minister of National Defence stated *for the first time* that an American B-50 from Goose Bay carrying a Mark IV nuclear bomb had lost its cargo over the St. Lawrence River.

Recent releases of previously secret documents from the Pentagon reveal that there were at least two other similar accidents *in the United States* during 1950. On July 13, a B-50 carrying a Fat Man bomb stalled soon after takeoff and crashed between the Ohio towns of Lebanon and Mason, killing the four officers and twelve airmen aboard and causing an explosion that was heard 25 miles away and blew a crater 200 feet in diameter and 25 feet deep. The U.S. Air Force denies that any nuclear materials contributed to this explosion.

Then, on August 5, another B-50 Superfortress carrying a Fat Man experienced propeller and landing-gear problems while taking off from Fairfield-Suisun airfield in California. The pilots attempted to make an emergency landing, but the plane crashed, causing a huge explosion that killed 19 aboard the plane and severely injured as many as 173 residents of mobile homes in the vicinity of the crash. The USAF attributes this massive explosion to conventional 500-pound bombs that happened to be aboard.

A Pentagon report on the St. Lawrence River incident in November of 1950 now claims the plane jettisoned an *empty* Mark IV (Fat Man) casing *and* three conventional 500-pound high-explosive bombs, the blast from which "was felt for 25 miles."

We will probably never know the bomb's exact point of impact, but it must have been somewhere between Cap-à-l'Aigle on the north shore and St-Germain de Kamouraska on the south side of the river, in a body of water 12 to 14 miles in diameter with an average depth of about 35 fathoms (210 feet). The high-explosive component would have detonated on impact. Since the "pit" had been removed from the bomb, plutonium would not have been involved but the uranium sphere must have been blown to smithereens and its extremely toxic dust scattered into the air and into the waters of the St. Lawrence.

One can only guess at what must have happened to life in the river, and on land beneath the prevailing west-east airflow downstream from the point of impact. However on January 12, 1988, *New York Times* correspondent Philip Shabecoff published an article in that newspaper about a mysterious die-off of beluga whales in the St. Lawrence which since the 1950s had reduced the beluga colony there from an estimated 1,200 to about 450. Pollution was suspected of being the cause, but the identity of the pollutant had not been established. Shabecoff's piece also noted that the region of the beluga die-off "has Canada's highest level of human birth defects, although no direct cause-effect relationship has been shown."

Over the years, scientists have autopsied more than eighty beluga corpses discovered along the shores of the St. Lawrence, and Dr. Pierre Beland of the St. Lawrence Institute of Ecotoxicology has reported finding "lesions of a kind never before reported in marine mammals, as well [as] tumours in numbers 10 times greater than normally found." And Dr. Lee Shugart of the Oak Ridge National Laboratory concludes the dead whales had been exposed to a substance "that would produce cancer in laboratory animals." Their findings were reported in Shabecoff's article, but apparently nobody has yet undertaken tests to establish what contaminants might have been involved.

Before the war, blue, fin, sei, and pilot whales were all present in the Gulf and in the St. Lawrence inland as far as the Saguenay River region. For many years *after* 1950, few were seen. And for some years after 1950, grey seals, harbour seals, and porpoises reportedly were scarce in the estuary, where previously they had been common. Additional anecdotal evidence given to me by fishermen, mariners, and other observers in the estuary and the Gulf indicates that populations of many species of aquatic or marine-dependent animals suffered significant declines following the explosion. These include several species of sea birds, herring, eels, salmon, squid, and sharks.

Between 1969 and 1977, I spent several summers on the Magdalen Islands in the Gulf of St. Lawrence. In 1970, the Quebec department of fisheries investigating the commercial shrimp fishing potential there found shrimp in abundance; but no commercial fishery was established because, the captain of the Quebec research vessel told me, the shrimp were "dangerously contaminated." The source and nature of the contaminant was unknown to him and so far as I know has never been publicly identified.

On the Magdalens, my wife and I noted a high incidence of cancer among the permanent residents, although there had never been any industrial activity on or around these islands to which this might have been attributed. Fishing and sealing were the *only* significant commercial activities, and provided the major source of protein for most of the *madelinots*.

One morning I came on deck to find the Gaspé coast in view, curving away to the southeast. We were "rounding the bend" into the wide waters of the Gulf of St. Lawrence, and the six-hundred-foot-high limestone cliffs behind Cape Gaspé were looming into distant view. Occasional clusters of tiny houses clinging to the shoreline below the massive brow of the Gaspesian mountains made me wonder how *les habitants* managed to make a living with only fish, trees, and rocks to draw upon.

Not long after I took the tiller, we sailed into the midst of a covey of dories bobbing a mile offshore while their two-man crews set and hauled handlines for cod. I altered course to hail one of the little boats and asked in my atrocious French if we could buy a fish. "*Mais non, mon ami!*" the man in the stern yelled. "We geev you wan!" with which he threw a glistening and still quivering ten-pound cod onto our deck as we sailed past.

Angus, who had taken the graveyard watch, was still asleep so Murray relieved me at the helm while I gutted the fish and took it below to cook cod chunks simmered in sea water with a few peppercorns and served with boiled potatoes, the whole smothered in melted butter. We did justice to it. Nothing of that noble fish remained for the gulls except the head and tail; I had sneakily cut out the cheeks and tongue to be later fried in diced salt pork for my own delectation.

Although sometimes disrupted by untoward events, our days afloat were following a steady pattern. Angus and I kept alternate four-hour watches, beginning at 8:00 in the evening and continuing until 8:00 next morning when Murray, who could now steer a compass course, would take the helm and handle the vessel pretty much on his own while we elders slept or did ship's chores, wrote up the log, saw to ongoing navigation, and repaired or replaced worn gear – a never-ending task on any sailing vessel.

Navigation thus far had mostly been from buoy to buoy, from light to light, or from landmark to landmark, a fairly easy task, necessitating only correct identification of the "marks" as shown on the charts or as found in the indispensable *St. Lawrence River Pilot*. We streamed the patent log during every watch. Our lovely brass affair not only told us how far we had gone but how fast. From it we learned we were averaging five knots. Angus claimed this was a fast passage but Murray complained it was as slow as the tractor-drawn wagon he drove on the Finnerty farm.

Most of the cooking was done on an alcohol-fuelled Primus stove as the weather was too warm for us to endure the heat from *Bonnet's* coal-fed Fisherman range. As I had warned him, Murray was the galley drudge and cabin boy, washing up and attempting to keep things tidy below decks – no easy task at any time and nearly impossible in rough weather. Nevertheless, he did his work with such enthusiasm that Angus promoted him from Ordinary Seaman to Able Seaman.

Here is how my father's journal described the way things were aboard and around his little ship, always referring to himself as the Old Man, which is what the captains of great windjammers of old were called by their crews, sometimes in fear and fury, sometimes in admiration.

*Farley had the first watch of the night and the Old Man relieved him at twelve o'clock. The breeze was light and the vessel just poking along at two knots. The sky was all ablaze with stars – too many and too bright. The Old Man did not like the look or the feel of the weather but settled down to watching the compass, a square of unsweetened chocolate in his mouth, his pipe close by while the vessel went her way.*

*The wind died down then suddenly came back and settled in northeast. The Old Man let her head pay off, away from land, and hardened the sails. In a trice it was blowing up no end of a to-do. The wind did not grow in strength, it arrived en masse, sweeping up an acre or so of spume all around them and sending* Bonnet *careening away on the offshore tack. The lights of some little Gaspé village flickered for a minute or two then vanished as the night became coal-black. The sea rose quickly and the tiller began kicking hard against his hand. The vessel bucked and pranced and flung up spray that burst in the crimson arc of her port-side running light.*

*There was noise enough now for anybody; shouts of wind in the rigging up aloft; the smash of her bows against the seas; and a disgusting clatter from the cabin where the kettle, Murray's dishpan, and sundry other things came adrift and fought back and forth across the floor.*

*Farley never seemed to turn a hair or waken, but Murray did. He scrambled on deck and crawled to join the Old Man in the steering well. He was in his underwear and shivered with the cold when the spray flicked him in his face, which was greenish-pallid in the dim light reflecting from the compass lamp.*

*"What's happening now?" he asked plaintively.*

*"Nothing, Murray. Just a hatful of wind."*

*"Do you want me to do anything?"*

*"No, thanks."*

*"Okay," he said gratefully and began to crawl below again. Then he turned and summoned up a grin. "I'll go back to bed if that's okay. Wake me when it's over."*

*And that, the Old Man thought, was pretty casual, and pretty stout, for a lad who had never been tossed about in a gale of wind before.*

*The way the sea got up, and the steepness of it, was a great surprise to him, an inland-waters sailor all his life. But the chart said there was 150 fathoms – nine hundred feet – beneath her keel and a fetch of 150 sea miles to the tip of Anticosti Island, the nearest weather shore. That was a great comfort since it meant they had sea-room enough that, if she didn't lose a mast or spring a desperate bad leak, they ought to come to no great harm before the wind blew itself out.*

*It grew very cold. The stars were gone and there was no sky, and the spume and spindrift tore by so close overhead that the mainmast seemed to be thrusting into it like a giant spear. And then Bonnet ducked her head and buried her face so deep in a breaking sea that the decks ran blacker than night and ripped the tarpaulin off the forward hatch so that buckets of salt water came through right onto the Old Man's bunk below.*

*The Old Man himself was now quite soaked beneath his oilskins and he was glad when his watch was over and Farley climbed on deck. Farley must have suspected things were getting rough for he already had his oilskins on, and rubber boots. He braced himself in a corner of the cockpit and looked around to see how things stood; then he began to grumble.*

*"You've wet your bed again."*

*"Yes, I know. What business is it of yours?"*

*"That's no way to speak to your son on a night like this. You are the damnedest man! . . . Look . . . there should be two on deck on a night like this . . . what's the course?"*

*"There isn't any. She's just going full-and-by but I think we're about twenty miles off the Gaspé shore. Maybe we should go to the inshore tack and see where she'll fetch up?"*

*So it was "Hard a lee!" and, like the excellent sea-boat she was, she never faltered. On the inshore tack now, the Old Man went below to take his rest. As he lay in his soaked sleeping bag staring up at the leaking hatch, he remembered some of the words of a sailor's song from long ago.*

*Fared we upon wide billows,*
*Cold lie the skies above.*
*Cold lie the seas below . . .*

*Next day the strength of the gale abated and the seas went down as they again approached the land. Then they coasted a mile offshore, almost in the shadow of gigantic, rounded hills where, here and there, a Canadien family clung to an up-tilted little farm and to the hard and meagre independence it gave them for reward.*

Toward evening *Bonnet* raised the improbable silhouette of Percé Rock, an immense, white limestone hulk with a mighty hole punched through it by the sea. The day was crisp and clear and the wind, from abaft now, drove us along so swiftly we were soon closing with the rock, whose splendour left us almost speechless, as Jacques Cartier is supposed to have been when in the year 1535 he stood on his poop deck gaping at this same spectacle, and could only express his amazement with the phrase "*Sacré bleu!*"

We laid course for the narrow channel separating Percé from the rugged, sheer-walled, and towering island of Bonaventure. As we drew close, the whole of the narrow plateau on its top and the innumerable ledges on its nearly vertical sides became a black-and-white blur of tens of thousands of nesting gulls, gannets, and cormorants. The stench of their droppings was palpable and the sound of their cries echoing from the cliff faces was almost deafening.

*Ahead of them* [Angus wrote] *lay a thirty-mile open-water crossing of the mouth of Chaleur Bay but they had the kind of wind only granted to the devout. What a sail it was! The seas grew high and came clambering after Bonnet, reaching up to swamp her from behind but she reacted to them happily and when one had passed under she would split the next one on her sharp Norwegian stern and never take a drop on deck. The log was giving her eight knots, a thing hardly to be believed, but it had to be because the fine old instrument, made a hundred years ago, was never known to falsify a fathom in its reckoning.*

*Halfway across, the Old Man remembered that the bullgine's exhaust pipe, which leads outside through a hole in her port buttock, was open. So he roused Farley and announced:*

*"We're going to stuff the exhaust hole with rags to make sure the salt water doesn't get to the engine head again."*

*Farley looked resigned. "We?"*

*"Yes. But Murray and I will do the hard part. We'll hold your feet."*

*They put a line about his waist – just in case – and held him while he stood on his head in the Gulf of St. Lawrence and pushed and pounded one of Murray's dish cloths into the hole. The hole is at the waterline, and the deck was high above. Farley was rather slow, and the Old Man scolded nervously. After each succeeding sea rolled by, Farley got a little air, then they could hear him swear. When at length they hauled him back aboard he was indignant. Salt water drained from his hair and beard and down his shirt and into his rubber boots.*

*"I stuffed it up her," he grumbled, "but it's all a waste of time you know."*

*"Why would that be?"*

*"Because you can't start your damn old engine anyhow. The batteries are dead again. Didn't you know?"*

*The Old Man changed the subject.*

When we began crossing Baie des Chaleurs, entailing several hours out of sight of land, we set a course on *Bonnet's* binnacle compass. This instrument had been salvaged long ago from a sunken Great Lakes barley schooner and was somewhat unreliable – so when we raised land again we were not greatly surprised to find ourselves ten miles off course and dangerously close to the New Brunswick coast. We clawed off, but it had been a near thing. During the remainder of our voyage we had to put our trust in a boat compass – a little thing one could hold in the hand, Boy Scout style.

Now the wind dropped, leaving us to drift idly through a perfect forest of lobster-pot marker buoys. Murray suggested we haul a few pots for a change in diet but Angus sternly forbad it.

"That would be theft, if not piracy!" he announced, making no mention of his conviction that lobsters are carrion eaters, quite unfit for human consumption.

We drifted amongst the pots most of the day until, as dusk drew down, we decided to find a harbour for the night. We had no luck. All the little ports within our reach appeared to be barred by shoals that would not admit a vessel of our draft. Consequently we were forced to spend another night in limbo, somewhere in the approaches to the Northumberland Strait, which separates the province of Prince Edward Island from New Brunswick and Nova Scotia.

With barely enough breeze to give us steerage, Angus and I spent a wakeful night avoiding lobster buoys and the occasional darkened motorboat that probably belonged to fishermen bent on poaching some other fellow's catch. When dawn broke we were fuming and fretting as we tried to identify something – *anything* – in a world now veiled by heavy mist. Finally, worn down by fifty-five continuous hours "at sea" we elected to steer directly for where we thought Prince Edward Island *ought* to be.

We were a bleary-eyed pair as the sky began to brighten. A light air sprang up to give us a push, chase away the mist, and dimly reveal off to port a shoreline that had to be some portion of Prince Edward Island's sickle-shaped, hundred-mile southern coast. I was at the helm so I pushed the tiller over and *Bonnet* obediently swung shoreward. The mist continued to thin and Angus, who was staring ahead through my old army binoculars, suddenly shouted that he could see the shore – *and* a small steamer lying alongside a wharf there. If there was water enough for a steamer, there would be plenty for us, so we started the sheets and *Bonnet* fairly bounded toward the land.

Smiling happily, Angus passed me the binoculars. I strained to see what he had seen – and the steamer became a row of fishermen's shacks and a ramshackle dock occupied by some lobster boats – which, I knew, drew only half as much water as we did.

We were sailing full tilt into shoal water.

I shrieked at Angus to take the helm and bring *Bonnet* about while I rushed to haul in the headsail sheets. As I did so, I glanced over the side and was horrified to see a cloud of bottom mud stirred up by *Bonnet's* forefoot. Leaping to the bow, I heaved our hundred-pound anchor overboard. Fortunately it caught at once, and as I snubbed the chain to the winch-head, *Scotch Bonnet* stopped abruptly only scant feet from driving hard aground.

An audience of five or six fishermen on the wharf had been watching this manoeuvre with great interest. Now one of them called out, politely wanting to know why we hadn't used the channel.

"*Because goddamn it to hell it isn't buoyed!*" I shouted furiously.

They forgave me. Two of them pushed off in a dory and, having helped haul up our anchor, towed us to where the unseen channel began and accompanied us to the rickety old wharf with the solicitude of a mother hen bringing home a vagrant chick.

Once we had been safely moored, they told us there *was* no real harbour at West Point, which was where we now were, and if the wind got up from any direction except north we would have to get out pretty smartly or likely be blown ashore. *Their* boats were all right here, they explained (a big smugly, I thought), because they could haul them up onto the land at the first sign of trouble.

They also told us we were the first sailing vessel to visit West Point in ages, and one of the few "strangers" ever to put in there. Their hospitality was overwhelming. All ten households adopted us but we became the special charge of Wendell Scott, who had been a lobster fisherman since he was eight years old. He had fished his own boat under sail for thirty years before deigning to install a primitive gasoline engine. Burly and indomitable, Wendell and his perky wife, Daisy, made us welcome in their home, a four-room frame cottage close to the shore. They lived there comfortably on Wendell's First War army pension, supplemented by his earnings as the community's unofficial taxi man (he owned the only car for miles around).

*The Old Man slept the night straight through never knowing that men stood watch on the dock, turn by turn, to awaken us in time should the wind get up from the wrong direction. It never did, but in the morning, Murray remembered something.*

*"Where's the boat?" he demanded.*

*"What boat?"*

*"The steamboat you said you saw."*

*"Oh," the Old Man said gravely, "she isn't here just now. She was second-sight, you know. She led us in."*

*Murray snorted. "I don't think there never was no steamer . . . sir."*

*Whereupon Farley roared, "Quiet, you farmer! You'll grow up to be nothing but another bloody sceptic if you don't watch out!"*

Both Wendell and Daisy were blessed with inquiring minds. They read as many books and magazines as were available, and every summer they filled Wendell's old car with camping gear to explore the world as far afield as New York, Cape Breton, and Quebec City. They had not yet gone to the far north but planned to do so as soon as Wendell finished building a boat capable of taking them there.

Meanwhile, they and their car were at our service. The day after our arrival, Wendell drove Murray and me to the village of O'Leary, five miles away, where the owner of the one-pump garage put our ancient batteries on charge, but could not sell us any new ones because he had none.

"Guess you got to go to Albert [Alberton]," he told us regretfully. "But while you're there, bring back the parcel of parts that's waiting for me and" – with a long wink at Wendell – "maybe something to wash 'em down with."

Wendell used the trip to Albert – only twenty-five miles, but an hour's drive because of the rambling nature and fearful quality of the red-dirt roads – as an excuse to give us a tour of the western portion of the island. Scenic it was not, being generally scrub-covered "barrens" with occasional rundown-looking strip farms mostly given over to weeds and potatoes.

"We get along pretty much on just three things," Wendell told us. "Lobsters, potatoes, and moonshine. The last two kind of go together, if you get what I mean, and lobsters keeps us from starving."

These fishermen-farmer-distillers built their own boats, round-bellied launches thirty or so feet long, open to the weather except for a small wheelhouse and cuddy up forward. They drew only two feet of water, an imperative in this region of sandbars and shallow harbours. Their engines were mostly old car motors locally adapted for marine use.

Usually two men, often a father and one of his sons, fished together.

We learned that a fisherman's work began in winter, building the half-cylinder traps that are about three feet long and made of laths and netting. The finished trap was thoroughly tarred to keep the teredo worm from eating the woodwork.

The men began fishing for the season's herring bait early each spring, hard labour, hauling and setting nets often in brutal weather. Vast numbers of herring were salted down in hogsheads (large barrels) and stored in fish shacks by the shore. When the season officially opened, the skipper and his helper loaded their boat and headed for their grounds, which might be from a hundred yards to several miles out. The best grounds were rocky shallows bordered by abrupt deeps, though lobsters inhabited almost all parts of the strait. Each boat set from three hundred to a thousand traps in "bunches" of up to twenty, each bunch carefully buoyed ("booeed") with a float that would remain visible regardless of the state of the tide. The vast expanses of water where the traps were set became jungles of buoys through which even a small boat threaded its way with difficulty.

With at least fifteen hundred dollars' worth of gear on the bottom (a single trap was worth at least five dollars), the men and their women watched the weather uneasily since a heavy northwester could destroy most of a winter's laboriously constructed gear.

Wendell took Murray and me to visit a little cannery at Alberton run by a very old gentleman with a rum-blossom nose and alcoholic breath. He showed us through his ancient plant with pride. Murray much admired the dexterity with which the packers – women and girls – tickled every morsel of meat out of the shells. Beaming with pride, the owner accompanied us step by step and was so pleased by our interest that he gave us six steaming-hot lobsters, which we ate while sitting on the running board of Wendell's car.

As we stuffed ourselves, Wendell recalled having once caught a giant lobster weighing twenty-three pounds that, unable to enter the trap through the entrance provided, had torn a way in with its claws. One claw, emptied of its meat, held a gallon and a half of water. He also told us of a man who once caught six hundred dollars' worth of lobster in a single day at the beginning of a singularly good season when "lobsters were as thick as lice on an old dog." Now, he told us grimly, there was "a fisherman for every lobster."

While in Alberton we met two young women from O'Leary who needed a ride home. They had just lost their few remaining, caries-ridden teeth to a travelling dentist who would eventually supply them with dentures. Their faces were as swollen as if pushed into a beehive and they were pretty glum, but they cheered up when Wendell not only offered them a ride but also promised to "find a little something to ease the pain." And soon after leaving town, he pulled up before a ramshackle farmhouse. He went inside and soon returned carrying a milk bottle full of a murky brown liquid. Some of this he poured into each of the toothless ladies, bringing grimaces and smiles to their sore faces. Wendell then offered Murray and me a swig. After one suspicious sniff, Murray refused, but I swallowed a mouthful of what was so nearly straight alcohol it would probably have burned in our Primus stove.

Wendell was a mine of information about the moonshine trade. He took us on a ten-mile detour over dusty red roads to show us a panel truck that, ten days earlier laden with moonshine, had been seized by the constabulary. It was now back in its owner's hands *and* back in business.

"They'll never nail that feller down!" Wendell said with satisfaction. "They dasn't dare: he supplies the most of the hooch the politicians use to buy votes come election time!"

Angus had not gone with us on our exploration, claiming he had chores to do.

*The Old Man was working at a borrowed tin washtub on the grassy plot in front of the Scott cottage, looking out to a sweep of reddish sand where children played, oh so quietly. They were not slow exactly, and certainly not subdued or listless. They had a poise that matched that of their elders, but they could fling themselves into the shallows with abandon and when they did the spray was bright in the sunlight and glowed for an instant with a red reflection from the underwater sands.*

*Out at the end of the pier Scotch Bonnet lay at rest, and Ronnie was at his self-appointed tasks. Ronnie had made himself ships-keeper. He was a lean, grave boy of twelve, silent, thoughtful, and strong as a good rope. The Old Man watched in some awe as Ronnie, on his hands and knees, scrubbed down the decks and white-work.*

Then Daisy Scott came out of her kitchen with two more steaming pails. She looked at the water in the tub and said, "You'd better change it now."

The Old Man did as he was told, and they fell into quiet talk. The kind that requires no effort to maintain; an easy and random exchange between neighbours. It drifted into talk of books, which came naturally because reading played a large part in people's lives at West Point, especially in winter time. This was a thing not in the least surprising. The Old Man had known for years that someone who lives with books will find talk about them everywhere, often far from pavement.

When the water in the tub grew cold the Old Man emptied it, removed the tub to the woodshed, refilled it, and gave himself a thorough lathering with yellow soap.

Then Wendell and the Old Man's crew came back after exploring as much of Prince Edward Island as could be done in a day. Murray looked like a boy who has fallen in love – a rapt expression on his face, and he was mumbling to himself.

"Twenty-pound lobsters!" he kept saying. "Six hundred dollars a day! Boy, I'm staying right here! No more farming in them burnt-out Albion Hills for me! Lobster fishing, that's the life!"

Wendell shook his head. "You'd starve to death once all that puppy fat was used up."

"But you said yourself . . ."

"I know I did. I said one man brought in six hundred dollars' worth . . . once. And that was a long time ago, before every spud farmer that could turn the switch of a gas engine got into the game. No, boy, you'd best stick to your little farm up in the hills wherever."

Yes, but there is another side to it. Later on the Old Man read Farley's journal for this day and it said:

"The houses are small and simple, set in red fields. It was clear the land was poor, but perhaps because of that the people had not yet lost *the need and the desire to work closely with one another on even terms. The people we met in stores, garages, and on the dusty streets of the little villages seemed to accept each other and us strangers as easily as if we were all relatives from the same family. They were not effusive, but they were sincerely interested in us and our problems and anxious to help solve them for us. I think maybe this whole damn island is one big neighbourhood."*

I suspect we all felt we would be glad to spend a year or so at West Point, but it could not be. Not only was our mooring exposed to every onshore wind but the tides in the strait rise and fall in ways no one can predict. We were told low tides sometimes *stayed* low for as long as twenty hours and could go low enough to dry out the wharf completely. Having no wish to see *Bonnet* stranded high and dry, we were becoming increasingly uneasy. Our unease increased as we heard horrendous new accounts of the causeway being built in the Canso Gut, now only about 150 miles away.

*The Old Man was quite convinced by now that if Scotch Bonnet entered the remaining gap she would most likely stick there in the middle and then be spewed back out again like a thrown-up fish some cormorant has brought back to feed its young. So he decided they had better get along while the getting was good.*

*Scotch Bonnet sailed at dawn and the Old Man never touched land on the red Island again. And will always regret that this was so.*

We laid course for Cap-Egmont, in Northumberland Strait, while almost the entire population of West Point stood on the dock waving farewell.

There was no wind, and after an hour the bullgine quit, leaving us to drift amongst schools of medusae (jellyfish) hanging just below the surface in wavering patterns like something in a science fiction fantasy. Murray watched them, fascinated, while Angus and I slaved over the engine, but without success. For the rest of that day and most of the night, we idled in a virtual calm until at 2:00 a.m. we got the engine working again – just as a fresh breeze came up.

Sailing again, we passed through a covey of small boats netting the mackerel that were pursuing schools of small herring, some of which, in their attempts to escape, went soaring into the air like flying fish. While I was on watch, several fishermen playfully motored across our bows, in effect challenging us for the right of way, but I was too tired to play games so I held my course until *they* gave way, grinning broadly at me as they passed. Later we were overtaken and passed by a little coasting steamer, a very old ship, very dignified and Victorian in appearance. Her duty, we later learned, took her to most of the little ports of P.E.I., then out to the Magdalen Islands and on to Cape Breton. I could think of no happier prospect than ambling around in her on one of her runs.

By early afternoon we were well down the strait, closing on Pictou Island, and the wind was rising. It was a dead muzzler so we spent four hours beating back and forth against wind and tide, making almost no headway until the tide changed, bringing with it a swelling sea that soon had *Bonnet* pitching about like a shuttlecock. A pomarine jaeger – an arctic gull that acts like a hawk and is very rare in these parts – came by for a look as we set course to round Cape George. Wind and sea rose inexorably and, as darkness thickened, so did the massive bulk of the cape, the northern extremity of mainland Nova Scotia. By then Angus and I were standing watch an hour on and an hour off, too tired to take longer tricks at the wheel. At 1:00 a.m. we finally rounded the cape and raised the feeble light of Ballantynes Cove, so packed with fish boats that there was no room for us and we had to moor along the face of the breakwater. The fishermen must have been surprised to see our big black hull when they came down to their boats at dawn, but they were kindly souls and kept their motors barely turning over until well clear of the harbour so as not to waken us.

We rose late, in this lovely little cove nestled under the forbidding mass of Cape George. A few farms clung to steeply sloping shores, and grey, weather-beaten fish shacks encrusted the foreshore. On the beach a few hundred feet from us was the rusted boiler of a tug driven ashore by a gale and, not far from it, the bones of a small freighter that had tried and failed to find shelter here from a hurricane. Despite these dark omens, we were delighted with the place. Angus sauntered off the dock, to return bearing gifts – three fresh mackerel for me to cook for breakfast. He was accompanied by a bevy of local men, one of whom, the manager of the co-op store, put his car to work ferrying cans of gasoline out to us and then refused payment for the use of the vehicle *or* the gas.

Later in the day I chatted with a pair of fishermen who had just returned to the Cove after spending six hours hand-lining for hake and cod off Cape George. They repeated the lament we would hear many times from inshore fishermen of the difficulty of selling their catches for enough money to provide a decent living because of the enormous quantities of fish caught offshore that were being dumped on the market by an ever-growing fleet of big draggers.

Our pleasant interlude at Ballantynes Cove came to an abrupt end when a fisherman peering over the edge of the breakwater quietly drew Angus's attention to our propeller shaft and its underwater housing. The stern bearing had come adrift, allowing the shaft to bounce back and forth in a way that would eventually bend the shaft and damage the engine or open a leak that could sink the vessel.

Repairs were urgently needed, but only a shipyard equipped with a marine railway could haul *Bonnet* out to be repaired. There was such a yard at Port Hawkesbury, halfway through the Strait of Canso and only fifteen miles from us, but the dreaded Canso Causeway lay between us and the yard – its opening now reduced to a couple of hundred feet, through which the unfettered power of the North Atlantic poured in a thundering tidal race. No vessel could buck such a torrent, but the Cove fishermen thought that, *if* we were very lucky and very careful, we *might* make it through at the turn of a tide.

We had a conference. Murray suggested we tie *Bonnet* to some safe wharf and proceed to Halifax by train. I thought we might try to make our way around the top of Cape Breton Island, but without a reliable engine this detour could take days and Angus had no time to spare. So, there being nothing else for it, we decided to attempt the Gut.

We took our departure soon after first light next day, under sail. However, as we met the sweep of the open gulf the weather closed down, bringing rain and southeasterly wind squalls right on *Bonnet's* nose. This gave us no choice but to use the engine. *Very* tentatively we started it up, and slowly, slowly *Bonnet* limped eastward. We entered Canso Strait four hours later just as a rising tide began flowing through it against us.

We had hoped to find a fisherman or some such water-farer here from whom we could get local knowledge and advice, but wind, rain, and fog seemed to have swept the strait clear of human life. Then, with fearsome suddenness, the ragged black mass of the causeway loomed dead ahead. Built like a gigantic battlement from hundreds of thousands of tons of stone blasted from a nearby mountain, it was pierced only by a gap that looked narrower than a two-lane highway, through which the incoming tide was already flowing like a mighty river.

At the sight of it, Angus reflexively hauled the tiller hard over, making *Bonnet* pivot like a deer encountering a panther in its path. We were circling, wondering what was to be done when a Norwegian freighter emerged from the mists behind us, running straight for the gap at full speed. As we watched in horror, she plunged into it with no more than a couple of dozen yards' clearance on either side. Though she must have been making ten knots, the current slowed her to half that. We watched with mounting apprehension as fountains of white water burst over her bows and washed across her foredeck. Then – miraculously, it seemed – she was through and steaming triumphantly eastward.

I glanced at Murray. I don't know about *my* expression, but his was piteous.

"*We*'re not going into *that*, are we?" he pleaded.

I glanced at Angus, who drew himself up and became a Canadian Captain Bligh.

"We've missed the turn of the tide. It's flooding now and it'll get stronger by the minute. In half an hour, we won't have the chance of a snowball in hell of getting through! Mate! Give the bullgine everything it's got. Stand by all hands!"

The current was now sluicing through the gap like "shit through a goose," as Murray later put it. But providentially an eddy had formed on our side and somehow we were able to claw up into it, almost scraping the rocks to port until we were within a few hundred feet of the curling lip of the overflow. Against all odds the bullgine continued to haul us ahead, inch by laborious inch, until unbelievably we were through! But not finished. We expected at every instant that the shaft bearing would go adrift, but somehow it held as we crept into the shelter of Port Hawkesbury's harbour.

A long, lean fellow standing at the end of Langley's Shipyard wharf waved imperiously at us. Jut-jawed and rakishly handsome Harry Langley, son of the yard's owner, took our lines, made us fast, and leapt aboard with a mock salute and a greeting that carried a sting in its tail.

"You fellows should be ten fathoms under! What the devil possessed you to try pushing your old barge through the causeway against a rising tide? Don't you give a damn . . . or don't you know any better? Ah, well. You're *main*landers, aren't you?"

He had been observing the causeway as we approached it.

"I figured you must've thought you were on a Sunday School picnic. I guess you know different now. Well, you've made it somehow, what can we do for you?"

My father's pride was so ruffled he stomped down below, leaving me to deal with things. After I explained our difficulties, Harry leaned perilously over *Bonnet's* stern, took a long look, then straightened, grinned, and said,

"Not to worry. We can fix that. And there's no need to haul your vessel up on our slipway – that'd be expensive. As you maybe noticed, there's a lovely big tide in the Gut. So just run your tub's nose onto the land alongside the government wharf over there, and when the tide goes out tonight she'll be high and dry on the bottom and our shipwrights will have that shaft bearing fixed in a jiffy."

Meekly we did as we were told, and *Bonnet* was soon securely moored at the government wharf, with additional lines strung from the crosstrees to the far side of the wharf to hold her upright after the tide had fallen.

While we were waiting, a rough-and-ready working schooner about three times *Bonnet's* size puttered down the Gut from the eastward and came alongside the wharf ahead of us. The name painted in uncertain script on her bows and stern read *Maggie Billard*. Her crew consisted of the skipper – a beak-nosed, bouncy little man of about seventy who introduced himself as Dolph (Adolphus) Billard – and his son Josh, who seemed about Murray's age.

Skipper Dolph told us they "belonged" to (and had just come from) La Poile, an outport on Newfoundland's southwest coast, and were bound for the Island for a cargo of potatoes, which they would bring back to the Rock and peddle to the scattered outports.

"But," said Skipper Dolph hospitably, "we's in no hurry, so come aboard, me sons, for a dram and a gam."

We scrambled over *Maggie's* splintered bulwarks to find ourselves aboard a ship out of another age. Every stick and timber on her was at least twice as heavy as it needed to be, and whatever paint may once have adorned her had long since vanished, revealing naked wood worn to a silvery sheen.

We followed the skipper down a steep and narrow companion ladder leading from a Spartan wheelhouse into a dungeon of a cabin that he smilingly called the "doghouse." Low-ceilinged, dark, and dank, it made Murray wrinkle his nose at the potent stench of ancient fish emanating from the gurgling bilges beneath our feet. Crowded into this malodorous little den, we sipped black rum out of chipped porcelain cups and listened, enthralled, as the two Billards yarned about life on their Rock and the seas surrounding it.

Angus eventually remarked upon the apparent lack of navigating gear and especially the absence of a compass. Skipper Dolph chuckled.

"'Twas like this, Skipper Mowat. We stripped the blades from our screw [propeller] on a trip into the Gulf and never had the dollars for to buy another so I traded me old compass for one."

Angus was incredulous.

"But, good *heavens*, Captain, how could you find your way without a compass?"

The skipper looked puzzled, and Josh answered for him.

"Well, you see, sorr, that old feller, he *knows* where every place is *at*. Don't need no compass, no, nor no chart neither, to find his way about."

The talk shifted to boat building, and Skipper Dolph described how he and his sons, with help from relatives and neighbours (the two terms are almost synonymous in a Newfoundland outport), had built the *Maggie* from timber felled "back in the country" and dragged out to salt water by horses and, when the snow lay really deep, by their black water dogs.

"Me maids [daughters] and me woman [wife] cut and sewed her canvas. Helped we to cork [caulk] her. And we named her for me eldest maid.

"Summertime me and some of me boys cruises round the Gulf picking up cargo wherever theys any to be had. Cabbage, coal, potatoes, salt herring, pigs and sheep – any old stuff as needs to go sommers else. One time we did it under sail but that's gone out. Now we does it with two or three old make-and-break, one-lunger engines rigged so as to keep the vessel going no matter if one of they gives up.

"Early spring and late fall we takes a full fishing crew and four dories aboard and goes after cod on Burgeo Banks or St-Pierre Banks. That be some cold misery when a winter starm blows up, but we's good for it and so is *Maggie*. Times we slips into St-Pierre dark of night so's the revenue cutter don't see hide nor hair of we, to buy or trade for rum or alky or black tobacco. Comes nigh to Christmas we might make a voyage to Halifax where goods is cheap and plenty, and bring home flour, butter, sugar, tea, and foolishnesses for the women and the young ones.

"After the Christmas jollying, we hauls *Maggie* up onto the land where the ice can't chew her up, and goes ashore ourselves. Wintertime we fixes gear, builds a dory or two, goes furrin' [trapping] into the country, kills a deer [caribou], has ourselves a time now and again – and makes babies. Them as is up to it," he added with a grin at his son.

Skipper Dolph reminisced about how, during the years between the two wars, he had shipped aboard big schooners out of Newfoundland and Nova Scotia, sometimes dory fishing on the Grand Banks; sometimes freighting salt cod to the Caribbean islands and returning north with cargoes of salt, rum, and sugar; sometimes carrying "made fish" (dried, salted cod) right across the Western Ocean (the Atlantic) to markets in Spain, Portugal, and Italy.

I might have been in *Maggie Billard*'s cabin yet had not Harry Langley come stomping aboard late that afternoon to warn us the tide had turned. We hurried on deck, to find the water had already fallen so much that the spiny sculpins that gathered around an adjacent sewage discharge pipe had left for deeper water. By midnight

*Bonnet's* keel was firmly fixed in bottom mud, and two shipwrights in long rubber boots were at work on her shaft by lamplight.

When the tide rose again, she was, as Skipper Dolph put it, hale and hearty. But although ready to go back to sea, she was not yet free to do so. The wind had dropped, and in the dead calm that followed, the world vanished under a blanket of fog so thick the end of the wharf was invisible. Nothing was moving in the Gut, and I was about to go back to sleep when the rumble of powerful engines brought me skittering up on deck to find a great black something looming over us. Whatever it might be, it was large enough to crush *Scotch Bonnet*. I was about to shout a warning to Angus and Murray when a mighty engine roared in reverse and a steel bow slammed into the wharf not five feet from us.

The newcomer turned out to be one of the big new draggers, fish killers extraordinaire, that we had been hearing about. On the so-called cutting edge of modernity, they were equipped with the latest electronic marvels, enabling them to get about in any weather with the certainty of seeing-eye dogs and to find and follow schools of fish at almost any depths. Within a few days their enormous trawl would fill their holds with fifty to a hundred tons of cod, haddock, hake, redfish, and several other species.

This one hailed from Saint John, New Brunswick, and was owned by one of the burgeoning international fishing consortiums. Her skipper was of a different breed from Dolph Billard. When he came out onto the wing of his bridge to watch his ship being secured, I hailed him from the wharf, but he barely acknowledged my existence. There was no invitation to come aboard, and no hint of an apology for the reckless manner in which he had brought his big ship up to a fog-shrouded wharf crowded with vulnerable smaller vessels.

When I went below again, I found Angus struggling into his clothes.

"What's all that foolishness up there?" he asked anxiously.

"Nothing to bother us. Visitor from some other planet. Noisy. And smelly. Not for real. Maybe when this fog goes he'll be gone too. Figment of the imagination. . . ."

I climbed back into my bunk but could not sleep. For the first time since our voyage began, I felt ill at ease – as if *I* was an alien in a foreign land. I was being given a glimpse into a future I feared I would not like.

I was drifting off to sleep when the lugubrious coughing of make-and-break engines near at hand brought me back to consciousness. This time Angus went on deck to see what was happening. He returned ten minutes later, shaking his head.

"You may not want to believe this, Farley, but the *Maggie Billard* just pulled out. When I got to the head of the wharf the fog was so thick I could barely see the captain only twenty feet away as he popped out of his wheelhouse to wave goodbye.

"'Come visit we when you've a mind,' he shouted. 'You and your woman and your young'uns. We'll make a proper time of it!'"

Angus paused and whispered, "He must have the second sight to go out in muck like this!"

He must have had because, almost nine years later when I took him up on his invitation, he was as hale and hearty as ever, and the *Maggie Billard* was still afloat in her home port of La Poile.

Later Harry came aboard bearing gifts – a steaming pot roast from his mother and a bottle of Lemon Hart from himself. At my father's request, he had also brought *Bonnet's* bill from the shipyard. Including the cost of three long-distance calls Angus had made from the yard to Halifax and Ontario, the total came to $4.50. He also brought us a proposal. If we would stay for a while, he would pilot us on a voyage through Cape Breton's interior maze of saltwater lakes that constitute one of the loveliest and most benign cruising grounds in the Western world.

Murray and I were dead keen to accept (anything to postpone venturing out into the vast unknown of the Atlantic) but my father had his speech to deliver in Halifax, and he was resolutely a man of his word.

When, later in the day, a westerly breeze blew the suffocating fog clear of Port Hawkesbury, the skipper gave the order to let go the lines and *Scotch Bonnet* sailed into the Gut and turned her bluff bows east toward the open sea. We had gone only as far as the mouth of Chedebucto Bay before the fog sprang its trap. A black wall of it rose up ahead, forcing us to tie up at a tiny wharf below the Chedebucto Lighthouse. We got our lines ashore just as the fog obliterated everything except the belly-shaking rumble of the defiant diaphones at the lighthouse.

The light keeper, a former lobster fisherman, came aboard. He was not able to sufficiently conceal his doubts about our seafaring abilities, and Angus was offended. So a few hours later, when the fog *seemed* to be thinning a bit, he ordered us back to sea. A bit of a breeze was making up, so we crowded on all sail and ran the bullgine at full throttle in hopes of rounding Cape Canso and reaching open ocean before the fog could smother us again. We almost succeeded. But the fog came back and then there was nothing for it but to steer due east, away from the hidden dangers of the land, and trust to the cold embrace of the North Atlantic.

A long ocean swell, probably coming all the way from Ireland, lifted *Bonnet's* keel and made her skittish. Somewhere off to starboard, a whistle buoy gurgled like a hungry sea monster. The charts offered no comfort. They showed the Nova Scotian coast as a wicked maze of reefs, rocks, and shoals.

The fog grew thicker as night fell. The swells became heavier and even I began to feel wonky. Angus and I stood short watches: two hours on and two off. Being at the helm was a tense business because we could see nothing. Once or twice the heart-stopping bellow of an invisible ship's foghorn chilled us. We could only pray they were equipped with radar and so could see *us* since we had not a hope in hell of seeing them until too late.

Being immured in that fog was like being engulfed in a void of darkness. Only the vessel's faintly luminescent wake and the flicker of the oil lamp on the binnacle remained visible. I lost all sense of direction.

Despite the heavy clothing we wore under our oilskins, it grew bitterly cold on deck. Our world, contained by the fog, seemed lifeless but when dawn lightened the murk a little, storm petrels appeared and danced buoyantly under *Bonnet's* bow like faerie spirits.

A little later a breeze began to freshen out of the southwest, and we prayed it would disperse the fog. When it finally did just that, we thankfully reversed course and *Bonnet* surged westward back toward Nova Scotia, now a considerable but unknown distance from us. Just before noon, Murray spotted a buoy in the waste of water to the westward. Angus and I joined him as *Bonnet* slowly drew close enough for us to read the name emblazoned on it: COUNTRY HARBOUR.

The land behind this buoy was hidden from us by shore fog but at least we now knew where we were. We were chagrined to realize we had only "made good" about thirty miles of the direct distance between Cape Canso and Halifax. Dead reckoning suggested that, in our attempt to escape the fog by sailing east, we had been headed for Sable Island – that sinister place a hundred miles offshore which seamen call the Graveyard of the Atlantic.

Sea and wind continued making up as we beat southward parallel to the Nova Scotian coast, "reaching" from one offshore buoy to the next – buoys that were anchored as much as ten miles from land and up to fifteen miles distant from one another.

Gull-like shearwaters skimmed the surface of the sea, never quite touching the wave crests or the bottoms of the valleys in between.

Angus wryly suggested they were as totally *in* their element as we were *out* of ours. Murray shook his head dubiously.

"How do you know they ain't just as lost as we are? If they're so smart, why don't they live someplace inland and give the crows a run for their money?"

A storm was approaching as evening closed in. Wind and seas continued to build until by midnight the waves were cresting at eight or ten feet, heaving *Bonnet's* twelve-ton bulk about like an old sack. Fierce squalls and driving rain made it almost impossible to hold a course. Chilled and exhausted, Angus and I should have been lamenting our fate. He didn't seem to be, and I certainly was not.

> *People at home would call us nuts to be out here in this. Funny, but I don't feel that way. Scared, yes, a little. Cold and weary, sure. But alive like I haven't been since the war, even out on the Barren Lands. I'm getting to sense and revel in what people like the Billards know about the real world and about themselves. I can begin to sense what the petrels and shearwaters and their like must feel about the sheer, bloody joy of living close to the edge. The satisfaction of being able to do that. Of being part and parcel of the real world and making the most of it! Crazy? Maybe so.*

Dawn brought no diminution of the storm. As the new day wore on, everything below decks not wedged in or tied down came adrift and went soaring and smashing about. Murray wisely sought refuge in his bunk – and was twice tossed out of it. Things were better up above, although the decks were awash most of the time, and when Angus tried to ease *Bonnet's* frantic motion by taking in the staysail, his crippled right arm failed him and he nearly went overboard – to be saved by the lifeline around his waist.

Although we yearned to be in some sheltered harbour, there was no prospect of finding one along that gale-lashed coast where every rock and reef must have been breaking white. There really was no choice but to again turn seaward and try to ride out the storm with deep water under our keel. (We would later learn that a hurricane was spiralling northward, making the eastern shore of Nova Scotia virtually unapproachable even to large, full-powered ships.)

Because we had no sea anchor with which to keep *Bonnet's* head pointing into the wind, we started the engine to give us steerage way, and the old brute redeemed itself by never missing a beat through the rest of this long night.

It was the wildest night I have ever known. Neither Angus nor I was able to stay at the tiller more than an hour at a time. When he relieved me, it was all I could manage to crawl below for a mouthful of cold water laced with rum, and for what seemed like only a few moments' sleepless rest, before having to tie my sou'wester back on and face the storm again.

*Bonnet's* motion as she laboured up the slopes of great combers and slid down their backsides became so violent that it snapped one of the inch-thick steel turnbuckles that secured a mizzen stay. Fortunately the other stays held firm, or a mast would certainly have gone overboard.

By dawn the worst was over. Wind and seas slowly moderated until we were once again able to set course for Nova Scotia – or where we assumed it to be. Overhead the storm scud blew away and flashes of sunlight illuminated the still-frothing surface of the ocean.

Hours dragged by, but still no sign of land appeared. I was at the tiller when, just before noon, I decided to stand up and have a pee over the side. Glancing ahead then I saw something the helmsman could not normally have seen because his view was blocked by the Carley Float lashed to the cabin trunk.

A few hundred yards away, in the middle of nowhere, a massive black buoy was bobbing about. Had I not seen it when I did, *Bonnet* might have run right into it. Painted in huge letters around its swollen belly was EGG ISLAND, which according to the chart meant it was stationed six miles offshore and just thirty miles distant from the entrance to Halifax harbour.

Alerted by my shout, Murray and Angus swarmed on deck. Angus was grinning with delight – until he swept the western horizon with the binoculars and failed to find any sign of land. Our hearts sank. Perhaps the buoy had broken from its mooring during the gale and was now off on its own deep-sea voyage?

Refusing to entertain such doubts, I scaled off the compass course from the charted position of the Egg Island buoy to the Sambro Light Ship off Halifax – a course that, according to the chart, would take us right through two air force and navy target ranges strictly prohibited to mariners. I did not mention these impediments to Angus, who was now at the tiller. I simply gave him the bearing to steer by and put my faith in the Old Man of the Sea to look to our interests.

We ploughed along for two tense hours when, quite suddenly, the shore fog lifted to reveal the jaunty, toy-boat shape of Sambro Light Ship, and Halifax sprawling in the haze behind it.

Once we were "inside the land," the temperature shot up thirty degrees, allowing us to strip down to bare essentials as we idled happily through coveys of trim little sailboats filled with pretty girls and dapper yachtsmen out for an afternoon's spin on these protected and salubrious waters. We felt *very* salty and superior.

We were received at the anchorage of the Royal Nova Scotia Yacht Squadron by a uniformed attendant who politely directed us to a mooring buoy next to a beer baron's glittering yacht. *Scotch Bonnet's* voyage ended here for Murray and me, although not for my father, who, after delivering his speech to the librarians, sailed on to New York with a new crew aboard, thence back to Lake Ontario via the Inland Waterway.

This was the last voyage Angus and his Dark Lady would make together. Two years later, for reasons still obscure to me, he sold her – and never sailed again.

Angus had made *his* eastern passage while mine had only just begun.

My love affair with the ocean and with seafaring people would flower and continue through the next decades and would carry me into many distant places.

And other lives.